WE KNEW
Jesus

BOOKS BY MARIAN HOSTETLER

African Adventure
Fear in Algeria
Journey to Jerusalem
Mystery at the Mall
Secret in the City
They Loved Their Enemies
We Knew Jesus
We Knew Paul

WE KNEW
Jesus

Marian Hostetler

HERALD PRESS
Scottdale, Pennsylvania
Waterloo, Ontario

Library of Congress Cataloging-in-Publication Data
Hostetler, Marian, 1932-
   We knew Jesus / Marian Hostetler.
      p.   cm.
   "Bible texts behind these stories"—
   Summary: Presents fictionalized accounts of the experiences of fourteen young people who knew Jesus.
   ISBN 0-8361-3653-5
   1. Jesus Christ—Juvenile fiction. [1. Jesus Christ—Fiction].
I. Title.
PZ7.H8112Wc   1994
[Fic]—dc20   93-5563
                                                                                            CIP
                                                                                            AC

The paper used in this publication is recycled and meets the minimum requirements of American National Standard for Information Sciences—Permanence of Paper for Printed Library Materials, ANSI Z39.48-1984.

Scripture is quoted or adapted from the *New Revised Standard Version Bible,* copyright 1989, by the Division of Christian Education of the National Council of the Churches of Christ in the USA, and used by permission. For references, see pages 156-157.

WE KNEW JESUS
Copyright © 1994 by Herald Press, Scottdale, Pa. 15683
   Published simultaneously in Canada by Herald Press,
      Waterloo, Ont. N2L 6H7. All rights reserved
Library of Congress Catalog Number: 93-5563
International Standard Book Number: 0-8361-3653-5
Printed in the United States of America
Book design by Jim Butti/Cover art by James J. Ponter

03 02 01 00 99 98 97 96 95 94 10 9 8 7 6 5 4 3 2 1

To Howard Charles,
my favorite Bible study teacher

Contents

Preface, by Luke 9

1. *Sometimes I Still Wonder,*
    by Reuben of Bethlehem 11
2. *My Cousin, the Questioner,*
    by Josiah of Jerusalem 21
3. *My Big Brother,*
    by Miriam of Nazareth 31
4. *His Eyes Were Kind,*
    by Deborah of Capernaum 46
5. *Where Did the Demons Go?*
    by Porcius of Gergesa 56
6. *Unclean?*
    by Janna of Gennesaret 64
7. *It Was a Miracle,*
    by Jason of Bethsaida 72
8. *I Hated Myself,*
    by Rufus of Caesarea Philippi 84
9. *The Light That Became Darkness,*
    by Korah of Chorazin 94
10. *Up a Tree,*
    by Jerusha of Jericho 102
11. *The King?*
    by Baruch of Bethphage 112
12. *The Plotting Priests,*
    by Jeruba of Jerusalem 119

13. *The Second Thief,*
    by Joanna of Anathoth 131
14. *You Can Know Jesus,*
    by Emma of Emmaus 146

Bible Texts Behind These Stories 156
The Author 158

Preface

Dear Theophilus,

How pleased I was to hear from you—and to learn that your grandchildren (plus a number of their friends) enjoyed my stories about the apostle Paul, as seen by some of the young people who knew him. Yes, you certainly are welcome to have scribes make copies of *We Knew Paul*, so that the stories can be more widely shared.

Now you'll see I have sent you, with this letter, a surprise. As you well know, before I wrote to you about the spread of the gospel (in *Acts of the Apostles*), I had collected stories about Jesus from a wide variety of sources. I gathered as many writings and reminiscences as I could from those who had known Jesus personally, in order to tell you about his life (in the *Gospel of Luke*). Recently I went through all this material again and sorted out some reports from young people. These accounts they had either written themselves, or I and my research helpers wrote them down from memories they shared with us.

My hope is that your grandchildren and their friends will read these stories (*We Knew Jesus*) as eagerly as they read the earlier ones about Paul. That is why I am sending them to you.

I'm glad Gaius has begun his medical studies in Alexandria. There's so much we don't yet know about our bodies and how they work, and so few people learn and practice what we do know! I have dedicated my life to caring for this human part of God's good creation—the body, mind, soul, and spirit.

My sincere greetings to the church which meets in your home—to those brothers and sisters I know, as well as to those I'll learn to know when we're together with the Lord in heaven.

>Your friend,
>Luke

1

Sometimes I Still Wonder

by Reuben of Bethlehem

"Ba-a-a-a," squeaked the tiny voice. It sounded more like the meowing of a kitten than what it was—the sound of a lamb that had just left its mother's body and had entered the world. Its little cries stopped when I connected it to its mother's milk source and it began to drink.

The night was cold and chill. Because of the birth, all four of us shepherds were awake instead of only the one assigned for this watch. Old Eben was in charge, as he'd been so often before at birthing time.

I'm the youngest shepherd and only a substitute when one of the others can't make it, and this was the first lamb that I'd seen being born. I thought of my baby brother, Joel, now six months old. We older kids had been chased out of the house when he was arriving. He too got his food like the lamb did. But from the very beginning, Joel could sure make a lot more noise than this lamb!

While I was thinking about babies and lambs, the other three shepherds began to settle down for a snooze, pulling their cloaks closely around themselves. It was my turn to watch. Usually there wasn't much to do during the night.

The sheep were all inside the waist-high stone walls, safe there unless some stray wolf or bear came down from the hills and was prowling around. It was possible that a human thief could be on the prowl, too. One of us needed to be awake and watching, ready to rouse the others if necessary. I'd never yet had to call for help or be called at night.

Sometimes, during quiet hours on duty, I'd think of famous characters from our people's past who'd lived in Bethlehem long ago.

There was Rachel, our ancestor Jacob's favorite wife. She hadn't really lived here, but when they were traveling, they'd stopped near Bethlehem because her labor pains had begun. She died when her baby, Benjamin, was being born, and her burial place and the pillar Jacob put up in her honor are still there at the edge of town.

Near our sheep enclosure is a field, the very one where Ruth gathered grain and met her future husband, Boaz, the owner of the field. They became the great-grandparents of Bethlehem's most famous son, King David. Our nickname is "city of David."

I like to think of how David, when he was my age, was a shepherd, too, working in these same fields and hillsides, and making up songs.

One of David's songs says that God is like a shepherd and we are like his sheep. While taking care of sheep, David became an expert in using his sling and in playing his harp—skills that made him famous and that we still talk about today.

Our group of shepherds is not so talented. But I do like music and sometimes try to play some of David's old songs with my pipe.

Another famous king is expected to come from Bethlehem—the promised Messiah. Many people believe he'll be born in our town. That's how they interpret what the prophet Micah said seven hundred years ago: "But you, O Bethlehem of Ephrathah, who are one of the little clans of Judah, from you shall come forth for me one who is to rule in Israel, whose origin is from of old."

I looked at the sky, soft and black, studded with the white glow of the stars. Some seemed to hang unusually low and were brilliant. Others were mere pricks of light.

Under my breath I hummed another one of David's songs: "The heavens are telling the glory of God, and the firmament proclaims his handiwork. . . . Night to night declares knowledge."

Suddenly one star seemed to be bursting open and streaking toward earth, toward me! Maybe I'd fallen asleep and was dreaming? Then the light was right there, throbbing around me, making the fields as bright as noonday. In the middle of the light stood a form, like a person. I cried out in fear.

The others were awake by then, sitting up and shading their eyes from the brilliance, frozen with terror. We were blinded by the light and were puzzling over words we heard. Later we agreed that this was an angel, a messenger sent from God.

The angel of the Lord noticed our fright. I guess they're used to that sort of reaction when they let people see them. The angel told us there was nothing to be afraid of. He had come to bring us good news.

"I bring happy news, for everyone on earth! Today the Savior Messiah has been born, here, in the city of David! You will know who he is when you find a baby, wrapped up and lying in an animal stall."

Before we had time to begin to understand what these words meant, hundreds more of these messengers from heaven surrounded us. They praised God, their chants filling the air:

> Glory to God in the highest heaven!
> Peace to those he favors on earth!
> Glory and peace in heaven and on earth!

The refrain resounded around us, echoing through the hills. Then, as suddenly as they had appeared, the angels vanished, and the brilliant light disappeared with them.

"The Lord's messengers—to us!" Eben exclaimed in an awestruck voice. "Let's go to Bethlehem and find this baby!"

"God has sent the Messiah to us—like it says in Micah!" added one of the others.

We all rushed off toward town. Partway there I remembered—I was the one on duty. I should be guarding the sheep. But I didn't turn back. This was the chance of a lifetime!

As we neared town, everything was quiet. It had seemed to us that the angels and their joyful cries had filled the sky. Yet the people of Bethlehem apparently hadn't heard or seen anything unusual. It was the middle of the night, and only at a few inns were there any visible lights or activity.

The inns were overflowing with guests because of all the people who had come to register for the Roman census. These were the best places to look for a baby in a stall, since town people kept their livestock out in the countryside with shepherds like us. About the only stables or animal shelters in town were those connected with the inns, where travelers could house their donkeys or horses.

So we began asking at the inns, "Do you know anything of a baby being born?"

The landlords looked at us as if we were crazy. Some people already consider shepherds to be on the same level as slaves and not too smart. On top of that, what a silly question we were asking at 2:00 in the morning!

Finally, at Isaac's Inn, Isaac gave some information. "A couple arrived here a few days ago. I was already completely full, but I said they could use the stable in back if they didn't mind. The wife looked like she was about nine months pregnant. Let's have a look."

He took a torch from beside the doorway and led us around the back. The inn was on the edge of town, almost up against one of our Bethlehem hills. At the bottom of this hill was a hollow with a rocky overhang above it. This formed a shallow cave.

A dim light from this shelter outlined the forms of

the sleeping animals—donkeys and horses, plus a few sheep and goats that the innkeeper would kill and roast to feed his guests.

We stepped over and through this living barrier which warmed the winter air entering the cave. Behind the animals we saw a man and a woman. She was lying down, thin and exhausted. He rose as we approached and looked questioningly at us.

"There it is! There's the baby the angel told us about!" I cried, pointing to a tiny bundle of cloth almost hidden in the pile of hay and straw near the mother.

She sat up slowly, staring at us. "What do you mean?" she asked.

Then we were all talking at once, trying to explain about the angels we'd seen and what they'd told us.

The man and woman glanced at each other. "Joseph," she murmured, a smile of wonder lighting her face, "let them see the baby."

He lifted the bundle and held it in front of us. We saw a tiny baby, seemingly no different from any other—opening and closing its mouth, blinking its eyes.

"His name is Jesus," Joseph declared. "Earlier we saw and heard angels, too. One told Mary he would be born, and to name him Jesus. And one spoke to me as well, telling me that we should name him Jesus."

We gazed at them and at each other in awe. Jesus was not an unusual name. But all our names have meanings, and this name means "Savior" or "God saves." Had the Savior really come at last?

"Thank you, shepherds. I'll always remember what you've told me about the angels' message to you,"

Mary said, smiling at us, and then at the tiny child she was now holding.

The next few days we told our story to everyone interested—and to those who weren't, too! Many were not impressed.

Others wanted to believe that the Messiah had come. One of the optimists was the mother of the innkeeper's wife, who made room in her house for the little family, so they could be more comfortable.

Things were nearly back to the old boring routine when the whole town was stirred up again. One night they arrived—a group of travelers looking like no others we'd ever seen pass through Bethlehem. I was in the fields again, and it was my turn to watch.

I thought it was only my imagination that the stars seemed unusually bright, and that one of the brightest seemed to be moving. Imagination or not, though there was little moonlight, I could clearly see the travelers who passed by our field, on their way toward Bethlehem.

The first strange thing was their traveling at night. People usually try to arrive at a city before nightfall—there are too many thieves and robbers prowling in the dark.

These men, dressed in turbans and jewels, would have made splendid victims. Their robes glittered with stars and crescents and other symbols, embroidered in gold and silver.

Such things are an abomination to us Jews. We are allowed to have some embroidery and decoration on our clothing, but nothing which is an image of something else.

What could these foreigners want in Bethlehem,

and how did such wealthy men dare to travel at night? Their servants, too, were richly dressed and leading some heavily loaded donkeys plus several tall humpy-shaped animals that I thought must be camels.

Afterward a servant girl told me what happened. She works for Isaac's mother-in-law. These men went directly to her house, found the baby Jesus there, and bowed down to worship him.

They said they had traveled weeks and months from a faraway eastern land to find him. We learned that they studied the stars and believed that stars could tell them things and make them wise. They claimed to have found a new star which was to lead them to a child, a child born to be king of the Jews.

But why would they be interested in a king of the Jews? I wondered. *Wasn't our Messiah only for us?*

Then they gave wonderful and precious gifts to the parents and baby—much gold and rare myrrh and frankincense from the East. These last two can be used as medicines and are also burned during our prayers—their fragrance rises to God with our prayers.

These exotic visitors left early the next day, heading back east toward their own land. People were quite excited. Some had doubted that this baby was special, but now their minds were beginning to change.

However, the very next day, everyone was stunned to learn that father, mother, and baby had left quietly during the night. No one knew where they'd gone. From the gift of gold they'd received, they had left a coin for Isaac and one for his mother-in-law.

Would there be no end to the strange happenings connected to this birth? Not yet, at any rate. Thus far these were wonderful events. But now came things horrible and terrible.

Soldiers from Jerusalem, our capital city five miles to the northeast, suddenly appeared at Bethlehem, sent by King Herod.

They surrounded the town and searched every house. They were looking for one thing only—baby boys. All they found, they killed with swords! My little brother Joel's short life was ended. They hacked him in two. Wailing and mourning filled the city.

Only afterward did we learn the reason for this cruel and dreadful deed. These strange stargazers from the East had been in Jerusalem before coming to Bethlehem. There they had inquired about a new king being born. Where could they find him to worship him? they'd asked.

The Jewish scholars that King Herod consulted told them that Bethlehem was probably where the Messiah would be born, and they had followed their star on to our town.

King Herod was expecting them to return and tell him about the baby who would one day replace him. His secret plan was to have this rival killed. But the stargazers didn't return to Jerusalem. They went back home by another way because they didn't trust King Herod.

When at last Herod realized that they weren't returning, he sent orders to have all the baby boys of the area killed—to be sure of getting rid of one born to be king. Did he ever know that the one he'd feared had escaped?

Now I'm old—nearly 50. I have often wondered what became of that baby. A few years ago I heard about a prophet that many people thought might be the Messiah—and his name, too, was Jesus.

This would have been thirty-some years after the events I've told you about. Could he be the same person? I doubt it. Instead of a being savior-messiah, this Jesus was killed.
 Yet . . . sometimes . . . I still wonder . . .

2

My Cousin, the Questioner

by Josiah of Jerusalem

When I was growing up, I used to see my cousin, Jesus, once a year. That was at the time of the Passover festival, when he and his parents (and later his brothers and sisters too) would come from Nazareth to Jerusalem and stay in our house.

Passover is the time when we remember how hundreds of years ago God saved our people from slavery in Egypt. Every family then needed to sacrifice a lamb and smear its blood above and beside the doors of their huts. That way the death angel wouldn't stop at their houses but would *pass over* them. That's why this feast came to be called *Passover*.

The people ate the roasted lamb and flat unleavened bread with their belongings packed and their sandals on. They were ready for the signal from Moses and God to leave Egypt.

So now every year, all who are able come to Jerusalem to remember this event. They eat lamb and unleavened bread together.

I was a couple of years older than Jesus. I remember one of the first times he came with Joseph. Mary wasn't along that time—she expecting another baby (James). They stayed with us as they always did because my mother was Joseph's sister.

At that time Jesus was about five years old, wide-eyed at the big city. Even then he had questions about everything. "Who lives in all these houses? . . . Why are that man's legs stiff so he can't walk right? . . . Why can't we go in the temple like our daddies do? . . . Who are those men with swords and shiny hats and short skirts? Why do they look so mean?"

Not being much older than he and not as curious and just as ignorant, I didn't have many answers. But I could answer his last questions: "Those men are Roman soldiers, and they look mean because they *are* mean! They like to eat five-year-old boys for breakfast!"

My cousin beamed at me. "Josiah, you're joking. I can tell!"

Every year when Jesus came, he was a little taller, older, and wiser—but he always had questions. Then came the year when he was twelve and could visit the temple and take part in the ceremonies there, as I'd been doing. Now he was taller than I, and he seemed quite grown-up in some ways.

He was smart but not a show-off about it, apparently a whiz at Hebrew. Jesus had long since learned everything he could at the synagogue school in Nazareth. You could tell he had thought a lot about religious things.

One question over which he was puzzling is this: Why do the elders say it is okay to help an animal in trouble on the Sabbath but not okay to help a sick person?

At my age then, I wasn't interested in such problems. I preferred to sit with my friends near our neighborhood fountain, watch the girls who came there with their water jars, and talk about them. Sometimes we played a gambling game, using pebbles instead of coins.

Jesus spent some time with us the first afternoon after they had arrived. When I asked him to come along another day, he responded, "Thanks, Josiah, but I'd rather be in the temple and hear the teachers there. If I had more time. . . . But I'm only here this one week of the year."

Off he went to the temple again. I was only at the temple once that week, because my father said I had to go along—to learn how to haggle with those who sold the animals for the festival. These had to be certified as being acceptable, normal and healthy, without any broken skin or bones.

When we finally agreed on a price and bought a lamb, we had to wait in line till one of the priests could kill our animal and cut off the parts they would keep for themselves. The rest we would roast for our Passover meal.

Because of rules our leaders made, to buy our lamb we had to change our Roman money into old coins minted in Tyre, a city to the north, on the Great

Sea. This money did not carry the emperor's image.

Our dads also needed the same kind of silver to give for the half-shekel temple tax. This was our part in paying for animals to be sacrificed and burnt on the temple altar. With these sacrifices, the priests would offer prayers of thanksgiving and requests for God to forgive the whole nation.

Jesus and Joseph went with us, since we were buying a lamb together. I never heard so many questions. The first trouble spot was the money changers. Joseph had to hand over his Roman coins which he'd worked so hard to earn in his carpenter shop to be exchanged, and so did my father.

From the changers they received coins acceptable in the temple. But the value was much less than that of the Roman coins—because the money changers took a big share to reward themselves richly for this service they performed. The value was reduced still further when the changed money was spent. It had no value except in the temple.

When the priests needed to buy anything in the city, whether bread or wine or materials for temple repair, they had to change the money back into Roman coins. Then the money changers had their second chance to profit from the same money.

The animal sellers also had to accept temple money and then exchange it for Roman money, so they charged more for their animals. Perhaps half our money went into the money changers' pockets, but it didn't all stay there. We knew that the money changers paid the priests well for the privilege of working in the temple court.

From all the money Joseph had scrimped and

saved since last year's Passover, he had barely enough to buy half a lamb, plus a few small coins left for a gift to the temple.

"But why do they have to have special money to use in the temple? And why do they change the money here?" Jesus asked. "Here, inside the temple walls? And they sell the animals here too! That doesn't leave much room for people who come here to pray. Isn't the temple for worship? And why do they charge so much to change money? That's like stealing!"

"Now, don't exaggerate," warned my father.

Jesus didn't want to contradict him, but I heard him mutter, "No wonder God says in Jeremiah, 'This house, called by my name, has become a den of robbers!' "

He was even more disgusted when he learned that the animals for sacrifice *had* to be bought in the temple. We were not allowed to bring a prize sheep from our own flock. And the price was much higher than if we'd been able to buy one outside the temple.

"Why do they have to be bought here?" Jesus asked. "Moses never said anything about that!"

The next trouble spot was where the animals were being killed. He hadn't seen that process before. The synagogues in each town are for teaching and learning. Sacrifices are to be done only at the temple.

"Why do the animals need to be killed?" Jesus wondered. "They haven't done anything wrong. I know God told Moses we needed this, but why?"

His eyes were troubled as he gazed at the long line of men. Each was leading a young animal toward the altar. Another line of men was carrying what was left of the carcasses away from the altar.

He burst out, "What does God really want? David says, 'Sacrifice and offering you do not desire.' And the prophet Micah says God requires justice and kindness, not offerings and sacrifices. So sacrifices shouldn't be necessary."

I don't know how he remembered all this stuff from the scrolls.

Now Joseph was the one who looked troubled. "My son, I can't answer you. I only know what we're told, and we try to follow God's laws as well as we can. Ask some of the teachers here who have spent years studying these things."

"I do try to ask them things when I go to hear their teaching. But I'm not really one of their students, and some of them don't like being interrupted with 'silly' questions. But they aren't silly!"

In spite of his questions about the necessity of sacrifices, Jesus carefully observed what went on as the priest took our animal and killed it. I saw his lips moving, but this time I couldn't hear what he was murmuring.

Now, years later, I wonder if then he had some hint, some idea, of how God himself would give one great sacrifice which would cancel forever the need for any others.

That year we celebrated the Passover together again, remembering that first time in Egypt and the freedom which followed. Now, although we weren't slaves, the Romans sometimes made us feel like we were.

The next day Joseph and family left to join the other Galileans on the trek back north. Two days later, in the evening, there was a pounding on our door. Father opened it, and there were Mary, Joseph, and the little boys.

"Is he here?" Mary cried.

"Why are you back? And who are you looking for?" asked my father as he brought them inside and tried to calm her.

Mary's eyes darted around the room, seeking someone.

Joseph explained, "We traveled a day's journey, quite a large group of us. Jesus wasn't with us, but we assumed he was walking with his friends as he'd often done on the way here. In the evening when we stopped, he didn't show up for supper.

"I wasn't concerned, but Mary was, so I went around to the other campfires, checking everywhere. He wasn't there, and no one remembered seeing him all day. So this morning we started back. We inquired at every likely place along the way. But really, we were convinced he'd be here. And now he isn't!"

"I remember he was with you when you left the house," I volunteered. "But if no one else in the group saw him, he must have soon left you—somewhere in the city."

"He wouldn't do that and not tell us," Mary insisted. "He must have been attacked by robbers!"

"Or stolen by the Romans," added his younger brother James, trying to be helpful.

We settled them down for the night, but none of us slept well. Joseph and Mary left the next morning to check with police and soldiers, asking whether any unknown boys had been found the last two days, injured or dead. No result. They weren't sure if this should be considered encouraging or discouraging.

"You know," I suggested, "he went to the temple to listen to the teachers there every time he could. And once or twice I heard him say, 'There's too much to learn in only a week.' Perhaps you should check there, and ask if anyone's seen him."

They agreed, and I went with them.

We entered one of the outer porches where rabbis would sit with their disciples gathered around them. Sure enough, we spotted him there, a youngster among older students and elderly teachers. We came up slowly and quietly toward the group.

Jesus was asking a question—no surprise! I don't even remember what it was—one I'd heard him ask before. More surprising was the fact that after answering him, one of the rabbis asked *him* a question. "If a person is born blind or deaf or lame, whose sin caused this—the sin of the person or of his parents?"

"Perhaps neither," Jesus answered. "Job's misfortunes weren't because of his sin or his parents' sin—but God's power was shown through him."

They were so amazed at this answer that they didn't know how to respond.

"Where does he get these ideas?" I whispered to his parents.

Then Jesus saw us and jumped up to come and greet us.

"Oh, I've been having the most wonderful—," he began.

"Why have you been so thoughtless?" his mother interrupted. "Your father and I have been anxious. For nearly three days we've been looking everywhere for you!"

"But . . . I thought you knew. Didn't you know

that I had to be in my Father's house, caring for his things?"

What did he mean by that? His father's house was in Nazareth.

His parents looked at him, puzzled. They looked at each other. Then Aunt Mary said a strange thing. "But... you're still only twelve..."

Then Jesus seemed to really see us for the first time, to return to the real world from the lively discussions he loved. "I'm sorry you were worried. I should have told you—asked you, if I could stay longer.

"We were all gathered by the temple, ready to leave, except for Aaron's family, who hadn't yet arrived. I thought I'd have time to just come here and hear a question or two. Then I'd hurry to catch up with the rest of you. But I... it was just so interesting..."

Joseph looked at him sadly and kindly. "I'd like for you to be able to study here. Maybe in a few years it'll be possible. But now—business is difficult, and with your younger brothers and sisters to raise, I need you to help in the shop."

"I know. I was only thinking of what I liked, what I wanted. Not that I dislike working with wood. I don't, but...

"Well, we'd better get back and start to work on those chairs for Nathaniel, hadn't we? I'm ready." Jesus went back to the curious circle of students and teachers who'd been watching us. He picked up his pack from the floor where he'd been sitting and told each one good-bye.

He never did get to study with the rabbis in Jerusalem. Joseph died a year or so later, and Jesus was responsible for providing for the family, with the help of his younger brothers. He wasn't always able to come for Passover.

When he did come to Jerusalem, he still sat in on some of the groups, learning what he could, but not with that open and childlike eagerness as earlier. Sometimes he'd seem discouraged afterward.

Once when we were alone, he told me, "They get so bogged down in unimportant details and think only of the words, not of God's purpose in giving us his commands. The Sabbath has become nothing but a burden for people instead of a time to relax and worship and be renewed, as God intended."

"That may be true," I agreed. "But don't say things like that in public, or you'll be headed for trouble."

"Yeah, I know." He smiled wryly.

But later he went his own way, *not* hiding his thoughts and—as I finally now believe—not hiding God's way.

We were both right—he in his ideas, and me in my warning.

3

My Big Brother
by Miriam of Nazareth

I don't remember my father, Joseph, at all. He died just before I was born. So my oldest brother, Jesus, then fourteen, was in some ways like a daddy to me. I had four other brothers—James, Joses, Simon, and Judas. They were nice enough, but Jesus was special.

Once he used scraps of wood to make some playthings for me—a kneading trough for making bread, a tub for washing, some water jars—small models just like Mother's big ones. I still have them, and now my little daughter thinks they're wonderful, too.

My brother had a lot of work to do. Yet he always had time in the evening to hold me awhile. Sometimes he'd tell us stories—such good ones! Often they were stories that he found right in our family or town.

One day Jesus asked Simon to go to Seth's shop for some small pieces of wood Seth said he'd let us have for a good price.

"Okay," Simon answered Jesus. But then his friend Thomas came, and Simon never went to Seth's. Instead, he played kick-the-ball with the other boys. It wasn't the first time Simon had promised one thing and done another.

Jesus didn't remind him and simply asked Judas to get the wood.

Judas was busy, working on a little cart he was making, and grumped, "No! I don't want to." But later he came to Jesus, smiling and loaded down with the scraps of wood from Seth.

That evening Jesus told us a story about two brothers. One said, "I won't," but did the work; the other said, "I will," but didn't. Then he asked which one had done the right thing. From then on, Simon began to try to do what he promised he'd do.

Jesus could tell funny stories, like the one about the woman who cleaned her whole house from top to bottom, hunting for a coin she'd lost. Then when she'd found it, she spent it and all her other coins to throw a big celebration party!

Sometimes he told mysterious shivery stories, like the one about an evil spirit chased from a house. But because the house was left empty, the spirit returned, bringing along other spirits stronger and more evil than itself.

He was the best brother possible, I thought. He was kind to everyone. He was good. He was patient and loving. As far as I could see, he was perfect. But not everyone liked him.

Some of the religious leaders in town (the teachers of the Pharisees) thought he wasn't careful enough about obeying all the rules. Well, neither was anyone else not a member of their group—and even most of those who were members! I doubt if even they could keep track of all the rules they had.

A few fellows the age of Jesus made fun of him, since his honesty and hard work made *their* products look shoddy. Another reason they were jealous was because nearly all the girls thought he was the greatest. Yet he didn't seem to notice them specially—he was interested in everyone.

Time went on, and he stayed at home, continuing as our big brother and our father figure. He was there long past the age when most young men and women, had, with their parents' planning (or at least their approval), gotten married and begun their families.

It wasn't because we lacked money to arrange for a bride. He and Mother had managed to find suitable wives for my other brothers.

Jesus was the oldest and ran the business. That and his gentle manner made him attractive to the girls, and he would have been a bigger catch than his brothers. Two of my sisters had also been married, and the third, Ruth, was betrothed. We were planning her wedding.

As for myself, I was now sixteen. It looked like my dream of being engaged to our neighbor, Caleb, would come true after Ruth's marriage.

I was glad Jesus was still with us, but I used to wonder why he didn't marry Rachel, for instance. I thought she would be a nice sister-in-law, and I knew she liked him a lot. But that was before I knew how *really* special he was, before Mother told us things about him which she had till then kept hidden from us.

It happened when the stories about a certain

prophet began to circulate everywhere. These stories, sweeping across the countryside, told how this prophet was preaching to the people. He was telling them to give up their ungodly ways and prepare for God to begin ruling again.

Some agreed with the prophet's message, and he baptized them in the water of the Jordan River. This was to show that they were washed clean from their sins. He said they would then be ready to receive the Messiah, who was to appear at any moment!

People from all over the country were going out into the wilderness to listen to him, near where the river Jordan reaches the Dead Sea. Many believed him and were cleansed or baptized in the river. People began to call him "John the Baptizer."

Our astonishment at these tales was even greater when we learned that this John was our relative—my mother and his mother were related. That was only one of the surprises Mother sprang on us when she called us brothers and sisters together one unforgettable evening.

I had noticed she'd been upset when hearing about John and what he was doing. I soon understood why. As we were sitting there together, she told us what none of us had known before—that Jesus wasn't really our full brother. She told us a story so fantastic that, frankly, some of us never could accept it.

I won't repeat it all here, as it's now public knowledge. It became public when Mother, after Jesus' death, resurrection, and return to heaven, told it to Dr. Luke when he was researching my brother's life.

Jesus was with us as she told the story that night. "I never told it all—even to you, my son." She looked at Jesus with love and respect. "When you were twelve, we told you some things, and when you were twenty, I told you more. Now I must tell everything. Perhaps this should have been done sooner. But now I know I can wait no longer."

She recounted everything, beginning with the birth of John the Baptizer, and the purpose of his life as told to his parents by an angel. Then she told about Jesus' miraculous conception and birth, and about the various messages angels brought to her, to our dad, and to some shepherds of Bethlehem. She included God's message about Jesus to people who saw him in the temple when he was presented there as a baby.

Could she have mixed things up, or through the years, added her own ideas to what had happened? She must have seen some doubts reflected in our eyes.

"No, it all happened just the way I'm telling you. I can remember each word perfectly."

With poetic rhythm, she recited the words of Zechariah (John's father); then the words of the angel to her, and her own words to Elizabeth (John's mother). She even knew the exact words that Simeon and Anna had pronounced when Jesus was presented in the temple.

"These are words from God," she assured us. "But even I, who have pondered them over and over for thirty years, don't yet know everything they mean."

I'd been so enthralled by this story that I'd paid no attention to Jesus and his reaction to it all. When I looked up, I saw that his place near the door was now empty. Joses noticed my glance and whispered, "He just left."

We didn't see Jesus again till two days later. Before, he sometimes felt the need for solitude and would go out into the hills alone for a day. But after this occasion, he was never really "at home" again in Nazareth. When he returned, he was different. He seemed so calm and sure of himself. Only then did I realize how restless and dissatisfied he'd been the last several months.

He spent a few days making sure my brothers understood all the aspects of the business. The way he did it showed them that there was going to be a permanent change, that this was a good-bye to the way life had been before.

When he was ready to leave, he told us, "First, I'm going to find John and hear him; then, I'm not sure of the next step, but I'm sure of being on the right path at last."

My purpose here isn't to tell you Jesus' life, but only to tell you a few things that I saw and knew of it personally. So I'll bypass his baptism by John and his stay in the wilderness and come to the time of my sister Ruth's wedding to Nathan.

That celebration was especially exciting for me. I was interested in everything she was doing, because I was imagining myself being in a wedding ceremony before too long. Then, too, I was eager to see Jesus again. I had missed him a lot, and we thought and hoped that he'd be back to take part in the wedding festival.

We had come to Cana, Nathan's hometown, and were in his parents' home, now Ruth's home as well. The day before had been the procession from Nazareth to Cana. Ruth had looked beautiful, decked in flowers and wearing gorgeous robes given by Nathan's family.

The rest of us girls, dressed in our best gowns too, sang and shook our tambourines as we danced around her on our way to Cana. We were especially active when we left Nazareth and when we entered Cana, but we couldn't keep dancing all the way, for the whole ten miles!

It was late when we arrived, and the first night my family stayed with my aunt who lived in Cana. She had helped with the matchmaking that had brought Ruth and Nathan together.

The next day was the short procession from my aunt's house to the groom's home. We arrived and found their house packed with guests. It was time for the real celebrating to begin.

About then I spied Jesus and ran to greet him. After his hug, I noticed he had a group of strangers with him. They were mostly Galileans from the lake area that he'd met in John the Baptizer's circle. Now they were traveling with my brother. I thought they seemed to be very close to him—closer even than his real half-brothers.

I guess that feeling I had was a foretaste of what Jesus himself said one time later on. When my mother and brothers had become concerned about his health and safety, they went to try to see him and to bring him home. He refused to come. Besides that, he told his followers that *they* were his mother and brothers and sisters, not us!

Most of the wedding guests never knew what happened with the wine on the fourth day of the festivities with three more days left to go. Even I, who *knew* what happened, didn't really know or understand.

Jesus wasn't the only one who'd brought extra

guests. Either someone had figured wrong on how many would come, or people were drinking more than usual. And even though the servants had followed our custom of mixing the wine with water as they served it, that evening the wine was nearly gone.

This crisis was the responsibility of Nathan's family and not our problem. Still, Mother was concerned. She didn't want Ruth and Nathan's big celebration to be ruined.

So Mother told Jesus about it. He'd always been good at problem solving. Perhaps Mother thought Jesus could have his friends go and find some more wine in the village shops.

Instead he said to Mother, "So what? What difference does it make to you or to me? This is not a good time for me to draw attention to myself."

I was ready to say, *What kind of an attitude is that?* But I guess Mother understood him better than I did.

She just smiled and told the servants, "Do whatever he tells you to do."

Well, Jesus didn't think of anything sensible. He told them to fill the six huge stone water jars standing there beside the house. They had to carry jugful after jugful after jugful of water from the well till they had the 150 gallons to fill those six jars.

While the servants lugged the water, they grumbled, unhappy about working at such a useless task.

Then Jesus directed them, "Take a pitcherful from one of the jars to the man in charge of the feast."

This steward tasted the "water." Then he demanded to know why the good wine had been kept to serve last rather than being served at the beginning, as usual.

Plain water drawn up from the well had turned into good wine! I even had a taste, so I know what I'm talking about. A process which begins with grape juice—not water—and which normally takes months, had taken place in an instant!

I didn't know how it had been done, and I didn't know what it meant. Somehow I didn't dare to ask. The men with him had no comments or questions either, at least none that I heard. They just looked at each other with half-scared, half-troubled expressions on their faces.

This wine tasted so good and was so plentiful that people drank quite a lot of it. Yet I didn't see anyone acting drunk. That puzzled me, then and now.

At the end of the week's celebrations, Mother and I and Jesus and his friends left, after saying good-bye to Ruth. With Jesus and his friends, we walked all the way down to Capernaum at the north end of the lake because Mother wanted to see where he planned to live.

This was to be his headquarters. From there he would go to the synagogues around Galilee, teaching and doing whatever God would give him to do.

"You'll come to Nazareth sometimes too, won't you?" Mother asked.

"To see you—yes. But I don't think people there will be able to accept me and my ideas."

He didn't explain any further what he meant—but we found out when he did come home.

* * * * * *

John the Baptizer was in prison now. King Herod

had John arrested when he had dared to criticize Herod for taking his brother Philip's wife.

Now stories were circulating everywhere about a new prophet. When he taught in the synagogues, his authority amazed the listeners. Besides that, he was miraculously healing sick people, too.

This prophet was Jesus, and we could hardly wait for him to come back home to Nazareth. Mother and I were so proud of him.

One Thursday evening Jesus arrived, and a few of his friends were with him. We had seen some of them in the group who'd come to the wedding. This time several other friends were tagging along, too.

News spreads quickly in a town the size of ours. Our house was soon crowded with neighbors and friends, come to see the suddenly famous hometown boy.

I guess they expected that he would be changed. They seemed disappointed to see him still wearing the same plain, natural-colored cloak and tunic as before and not making any effort to show off or dominate the conversation.

I was sitting beside Jesus and observed two incidents I want to tell you about. Not everyone noticed them. The first was when Zack approached him. He was a man about Jesus' age, although he looked older. His face was lined and hard looking, his clothing careless and not too clean. A dirty bandage covered most of one arm.

Zack boldly started the conversation. "Well, Jeez, old pal, I hear you're supposed to be a great healer now. How about demonstrating what you can do? If you'd heal this here broken arm of mine, I could get back to work!"

He was a stone mason by trade but wasn't noted for doing much work.

"Your arm will heal if you take care of it," Jesus calmly stated. "But you know what caused your broken arm. If you have any love for your family, you should change your ways—before something worse happens."

He gave Jesus a surprised look, then muttered viciously, "You mind your own business!" and stalked away.

I hadn't even heard yet about his broken arm or the cause, so how could Jesus have known already? Later I heard rumors that he'd been drunk and the arm had been broken when he'd gotten into a fight at a prostitute's house.

The other event had to do with little Clea, our neighbor's eight-year-old daughter. Ever since she was two and had been very sick with a fever, she'd had sore and swollen joints—especially her fingers, elbows, and knees.

This gradually became worse, and now Clea could hardly move around, and then only with much pain. Yet she usually managed to be cheerful and had been a great favorite with Jesus.

Jesus saw Clea peering at him from behind the bigger people crowding around. He went to get her and placed her on his lap, talking softly to her. Jesus was asking her about her pet goat and about her big brother and sister. All the while he was gently rubbing her fingers and placing his hands over her swollen knees and elbows.

"How would you like to have your arms and legs working better?" he asked her.

41

"I'd like it," she admitted shyly. "Can you help them? Mommy said you could, but that I mustn't pester you about it."

"Well, what do you think?" Jesus asked. "How about your arm? Try to wiggle it. Doesn't it feel a little better now?"

She carefully moved her left arm. She seemed to be able to move it farther and more easily than before.

"Yes, I think so!" she exclaimed.

Jesus took her hand and led her over to where her mother was waiting. Clea was able, with his help, to use her legs somewhat. From then on it was a gradual healing. After several months, she could move almost normally.

These two quiet incidents show both the mocking unbelief and the faith which were present at Nazareth. They show why it was said later about his visit to our town, "He could do no deed of power there, except that he laid his hands on a few sick people and cured them."

What the whole town was really waiting for was to see what would happen on the Sabbath in the synagogue. This person had grown up here, and what would he have to say to his own people?

My brothers envied Jesus for all the attention he was getting. Joses razzed him, "Here's your chance to show your stuff."

On Saturday the synagogue was packed long before starting time. Why did the people come? Did they expect to be made proud by seeing one of their own who'd made good? Perhaps they came hoping to see him flop, so they could say, *I knew it. He's still only a common carpenter after all.*

I guess some of each type were there. And each group saw and heard what they wanted to see and hear.

After the opening prayer and chants, Jesus stood up on the platform. As a visiting teacher, they asked him to read the Scriptures, and then he could also comment on the passage.

Reverently the attendant placed the scroll of Isaiah on the table in front of Jesus, who unrolled it to find the place he wanted. He read (recited really—he knew the words by heart), looking into our eyes:

> The Spirit of the Lord is upon me
> > because he has anointed me
> > > to bring good news to the poor.
> He has sent me to proclaim release
> > to the captives
> > > and recovery of sight to the blind,
> > to let the oppressed go free,
> > > to proclaim the year of the Lord's favor.

Then he rerolled the scroll, returned it to the attendant, and sat down on what we call Moses' seat, for the one who teaches. The first thing Jesus said really grabbed our attention: "Today this Scripture has been fulfilled in your hearing."

It could mean only one thing—he was claiming to be the Messiah sent by God to be our Savior and deliverer! It was just as Mother had told us.

Jesus continued speaking in such a way that everyone was amazed. I could hear the whispers around me:

"What a speaker! I never heard the like!"

"Joseph's son—one of our own—maybe the Messiah!"

"What words of grace!"

Well, that amazed approval didn't last long. Some complained:

"Why didn't he read the next line from Isaiah, about God's day of vengeance on the other nations? It's high time they get what's coming to them!"

"What would a local boy know, anyhow? With what teacher did he study?"

If only Jesus had stopped there, instead of criticizing the people of Nazareth! He went on:

"Doubtless you'll quote to me this proverb, 'Doctor, cure yourself!' And you'll say, 'Do here also in your hometown the things that we've heard you did at Capernaum.' Truly I tell you, no prophet is accepted in the prophet's hometown."

Murmurs of protest began. But he hadn't finished yet. There was worse to come!

"There were many widows in Israel in the time of Elijah, when there was no rain for three years and six months, and there was a severe famine over all the land. Yet Elijah was sent to none of the Israelite widows but to a widow at Zarephath in Sidon.

"There were also many lepers in Israel in the time of the prophet Elisha, and none of them was cleansed, but Naaman the Syrian was."

I thought, *Even if everything he says is true, does he have to say it all right here?*

Yes, God through his prophets had helped those two pagans, the widow from Sidon and Naaman from Syria, rather than helping some of his own Israelite people. But this was something the people of Nazareth weren't prepared to accept or to hear.

Yet it took some leaders to help stir up the people

from anger to physical violence. I think Zack was a ringleader. They surrounded Jesus and forced him out of the synagogue. Soon everyone was out on the street, the women pouring out after the men, and we were swept along too.

The angry worshipers had turned into a murderous mob which rushed through the streets, out of town, and on up to the top of the hill.

We were almost last and couldn't tell what was happening further along. Were they going to stone him? That form of punishment still happened occasionally, but never in Nazareth that I knew of.

The crowd, pushing and shoving, gathering force, was still climbing toward the point where there was a ledge and sharp drop-off, a cliff overlooking the valley far below.

We were too far back to see what was happening, but we could hear shouting:

"Away with him!"

"Throw him over the edge!"

"Death to the blasphemer!"

I was sure I recognized Zack's voice among them.

I don't know yet how Jesus escaped. Something turned the raging mob into a group of shamefaced people, looking everywhere but at him. I guess it was God's power protecting him.

Anyhow, Jesus passed through the silent crowd, headed not back to town but toward Capernaum. He said nothing to anyone, but smiled grimly at Mother and me as he walked by.

The road he took didn't lead him to safety, though, not in the end. Yet it led him the way he had to go. How little did we then understand that way, or him!

4

His Eyes Were Kind
by Deborah of Capernaum

There was quite a hubbub in the synagogue this morning. I wish I could have been there, but Grandma's sick, and I had to stay home and help Mother. There wasn't much to do so far as the food was concerned. We had prepared all we could yesterday so as not to do it today, on the Sabbath.

Dad's friend, Jesus, will be here for the noon meal. We haven't met him yet, but when Dad went to see John the Baptizer and hear his preaching, he met this man, and it's been "Jesus, this . . . Jesus, that" till I'm tired of hearing the name.

Mother's not too happy about this friendship, either. Ever since Dad met Jesus, he's been away from home a lot, going here and there with Jesus and his band. Uncle Andrew is just as bad. In fact, he started the whole thing by introducing Dad to Jesus.

Dad's business is fishing. When he's gone, that means less fishing gets done and less money comes in. We can't depend on Dad's partners any more, either—James and John, the sons of Zebedee. They're also excited about this new . . . what? Prophet? Teacher? Messiah? I don't know! Maybe I'll find out more later.

Anyway, about this morning—my friend Zina stopped by on her way home from synagogue to tell us what happened. A lot of people were there, even crazy old Barak. In his saner moments he claims an evil spirit possesses him and causes him to do the nutty things he does.

We all know *he* hardly ever comes to the synagogue. If he really had an evil spirit in him, would he come to the synagogue? Yet when Jesus was reading the Scripture, Barak jumped up and shouted in an awful, wild voice, "Let us alone! Jesus of Nazareth, what have you to do with us? Did you come to destroy us?"

It was the demon speaking through Barak. Then he cried in his normal voice, "I know you. You're the Holy One of God!"

Zina said it was really weird. It made the chills run up her back to hear those two different voices coming out of the same mouth.

Then Jesus firmly told the evil spirit, "Be silent, and come out of him!"

The unclean spirit threw Barak down to the floor in a convulsion. Then it must have left him, because Barak quietly got up and sat down, apparently more himself than he'd been for years.

People were really impressed by what Jesus had done, and everyone was discussing his power and authority. Still, some were wondering if it was right for him to heal on the Sabbath. That was breaking the rules.

Well, I want to see for myself—both Jesus and the new Barak—before I decide.

* * * * * *

It's a day later than when I began my story. Now I *have* seen for myself—plenty! Zina had barely left when Dad and Andrew came in, with James and John—*and Jesus.* When I first saw him I thought, *What's all the fuss about? He doesn't look like anyone special to me.*

But that was before he greeted me, before he helped Grandma, before . . . all the other things I'm going to tell you about. He had something special to say to each of us four kids, from one-year-old Simon, Junior, to me, the oldest, as Dad introduced us to him.

"Your dad's told me a lot about you, Deborah," he commented to me. "He's proud of the way you help your mother, especially now that he's been spending some time away from home—with me."

His eyes were what I noticed most as I talked to him. They were so kind. They seemed to look right inside me, without being disgusted at the selfishness and weaknesses they could see there. I sensed that Jesus was accepting it all with love.

I was thinking, *He's so kind. . . . I could tell him how hard it's getting for us with Dad gone so much. He'd understand.*

Before I could begin to express my thoughts, he answered them! "Don't worry about what you'll eat or drink or wear. God takes care of the birds. He takes care of the flowers. And you're worth a lot more to him than they are!"

Then he gave me a special smile and added, "I'm thinking of something—you'll find out later what my idea is, and then you'll remember what I said . . . and understand."

His specialness even affected my skeptical mother. She pulled back the curtain shielding the corner of the room where Grandma was lying. She looked worse than before, and her body was shaking from the fever. I thought her headache must be worse, too. She was moaning, and her robe and bedclothes were wet from sweating.

"This is my mother," Mother told Jesus. "Can you help her? She's had this fever for four days and is getting worse. I don't know what to do!"

Jesus looked at Grandma for an instant. Then he took her thin weak hand in his strong one and placed his other hand on her forehead. He murmured something, but I couldn't hear for certain what. I thought maybe he said, "Go. Now." And then he pulled her toward a sitting position.

All at once her eyes were bright and clear. She almost jumped out of bed, and instead of moaning, she began to talk in her usual brisk and bossy way. "Why's everyone just standing around? I believe we have guests here, and it's lunchtime!"

Out Grandma went to the cooking room and began to carry in the food and serve it! It was almost funny!

"Grandma, are you really okay?" I asked as I went to help serve also.

"Huh, just feel my forehead, Deborah," she

snapped. It was as cool as if she'd never had that burning fever! I didn't hear her say thanks to Jesus. But she showed she knew what had happened by giving him extra portions of everything and hovering about him to refill his cup or to supply whatever he might need.

This cure plus the morning's big event at the synagogue had stirred up the whole town with excitement. Evening came, and the setting sun signaled the end of Sabbath—and the end of the restrictions on walking or healing, or on any other work.

A crowd began to gather outside our door. More and more people came, bringing friends or family members sick with diseases or with evil spirits.

I saw some people I knew about: Nathan's father and Sarah's younger sister, both of whom had fevers like Grandma's. The crazies, afflicted like Barak had been. Barak, almost unrecognizable now that he was in his right mind. He was bringing a man named Enoch, in worse condition than Barak had been.

I also saw many that I didn't know, sick in their bodies or sick in their minds—or both. As I watched, Jesus touched each one and talked to each one. I saw fevers disappear. People who needed to be helped or carried to our doorway were able to walk away unaided.

I saw the possessed and heard their demons screaming in rage and fear. Some shouted "You are the Son of God!" But Jesus sternly told them not to say that. He commanded those spirits to leave the bodies of the people they had been tormenting.

What else can I say? I can only tell you what I saw that evening and the happiness which came to many families through what Jesus did.

* * * * * *

I want to report one more incident which happened a few days later. I was a part of it.

There weren't many sick people around any more—most had been healed! But there were still crowds. They wanted to hear Jesus talk about God, whom he called our heavenly Father.

Jesus had an endless supply of stories, some short, some longer. Each one had a point, to teach us more about God and his ways. Yet often the stories were puzzling, and we weren't quite sure what the point was.

If someone asked, he'd usually just say, "Let those who want to hear, listen." Then when most of the people got restless and wandered off, he'd explain the hard-to-understand stories to those who were really interested and who had lingered behind.

During this time Dad and his partners were trying to get in some fishing but weren't having much luck. Once more they'd gone out at night, hoping for a good catch. The next morning we'd eaten breakfast, and they hadn't returned yet.

Jesus turned to me. "Let's go down to the lake, Deborah, and see if they're back and how they've done."

Of course, I agreed. By then I would have been glad to go anywhere with him.

Well, we don't live far from the lake, but before we got there, people had spotted Jesus and were flocking along after us. We didn't have a chance to check with Dad. They were swarming around us, elbowing each other, asking questions, demanding stories. They almost pushed us into the water.

Dad's boat was right next to us. I saw it was completely empty of any kind of fish. He and Andrew and their helpers were nearby, washing the seaweed out of the nets.

I waded over to Dad. "Still no luck?" I asked.

"Nothing," he muttered with a worried look.

"Simon, come here."

Jesus was calling Dad. He was climbing into the boat as Dad walked over to it. "Would you please push the boat out a little way from the shore? It's impossible to talk to people when they're crowding around us like this."

I hopped in too, and Dad pushed us a few yards into the water. *A neat idea,* I thought. Jesus had a place to sit and space to breathe and move. The people could sit on the bank, the sand, or the rocks. This way they could hear better than when they were struggling and vying with each other to be closer.

Two of his stories that day had to do with the sea. He said God's kingdom is like a precious pearl. (Pearls come from sea animals like clams, mostly in saltwater seas rather than in our little lake). A merchant searching for fine pearls sees this extra-special one. He wants it so much that he sells everything else he has to get this one pearl.

Then Jesus compared God's kingdom to pulling in a fishing net filled with all kinds of fish—some good to eat and some not. So the fishers sort them out—throwing away the bad ones and keeping the good ones. He said that's like the end of the world, when the angels will separate the good people from the bad.

Do you understand all this? I don't think I do. I'm

not sure anyone can completely figure them out. But his stories make us think and make us want to learn more about God.

Then he told the people good-bye and sent them away to go about their daily work. They weren't all ready to leave—so we left them! By then Dad had finished cleaning the nets and had brought them to the boat.

Jesus directed him, "Head out to the deep water, and let down your nets for a catch."

Dad sighed, "All night long we had our nets down. We worked hard—and caught absolutely nothing. But if you say so," he grudgingly agreed, "we'll do it."

I was so excited to be along. I'd seldom been allowed to go before. They usually went out at night, and fishing wasn't thought to be for girls, even in the daytime.

They let out the sail, and we were soon bouncing over the waves and beyond the shallow water. Then they took down the sail and threw out the nets. All at once the blue water was churning and flashing from the movement of hundreds of fish!

"Pull the nets in, fellows, pull them in!" Dad shouted.

Together Dad and one helper pulled on one net, while Andrew and the other man pulled the other net.

"I've never done this before—I'm just a carpenter," commented Jesus. He was smiling broadly as he bent over to help pull.

"Me neither!" I exclaimed as I tried to add my bit of strength at the other net. But the nets were so loaded we could barely move them!

"I don't believe this!" panted Dad. "The nets are

starting to tear from the weight of the fish!"

Dad began signaling frantically for help from James and John, back on shore. In their boat they set out to rescue us.

With all of us working together, we pulled the nets in and emptied them, one into each boat. But there were so many fish and they were so heavy that the boats were about to be swamped! I was sure we were all going to sink and drown!

Dad looked dazed. He knelt down by Jesus and asked, "Lord, what do you want with me? I'm just a sinful fisherman. Let me be!"

"Don't be afraid," Jesus encouraged him. "From now on you'll be fishing for people."

Somehow, even though we were so low in the water that the smallest wave splashed over the side of the boats, we made it back to shore.

From then on James and John, and Andrew and Dad went with Jesus whenever and wherever he went, "fishing for people"—whatever that meant! Their boats weren't idle. Their helpers tried to carry on as well as they could.

The day of the huge catch, we were incredibly busy. We sold in town what fish we could, but that was just a small fraction of them. The others had to be cleaned and then dried or salted or pickled to preserve them. Preserved fish from our lake are sold as far away as Rome and are traded by Galilean merchants to many other places too.

So our income received an enormous boost at just the time it was needed—when our main income-earner was gone. And then I remembered how Jesus had told me that first day not to worry about money and such things. I was sure now that I knew what his idea was—the idea that he said I'd find out about later!

5

Where Did the Demons Go?

by Porcius of Gergesa

Even though I didn't particularly like my job, I never dreamed that one day I'd be working as usual, watching the pigs, and the next day I'd be out of work—no more pigs, no more herding. And what a way to lose a job! I'll bet no other swineherds ever lost their jobs the way we did—no, nor ever will!

There were two hundred pigs in the herd, and about fifty belonged to my boss, Philo. Each of the five owners had a way of marking his own pigs—a nick in the ear or tail or a sign stained on the animals' hind quarters. Each owner sent herders to watch over his own animals. We worked together—more or less. I was the youngest, just an apprentice, still learning.

Pigs will eat grass, but they aren't as fond of it as

sheep and cattle are. Neither do they eat everything in sight like goats do. So sometimes we would round up something extra for them—like the chaff left at threshing time (mixed with water, they thought it was a treat), or the seed pods produced by thorny carob trees. We would let them scrounge almost anywhere for bulbs and acorns and garbage.

Occasionally our owners would ask us to pick out a nice piglet to sacrifice in a ritual to make things pure after something evil happened, or to prepare for a public assembly. Other times they wanted a pig to sacrifice to one of the gods of the underworld.

Another of our tasks was to see that the pigs stayed away from Gergesa. Most of us living in the town are Greeks. But there are a few Jews, and they get terribly upset if they even *see* a pig in the distance! It seems silly to me—but their religion teaches them that pigs are unclean and that they mustn't eat anything connected with them.

Well, that's okay with me. Jews don't *have* to eat pigs. Excuse me while I think about crisp bacon, tender slices of ham, succulent roast pork. It just doesn't make sense to me, especially after one of their boys getting ready for his son-of-the-law ceremony told me that their God created everything, and it is all good.

Two hundred pigs take a lot of feeding to get them to a good weight for butchering and selling. We had already grazed the best places around, over and over. So the day I lost my job, there was no other choice left. We had to take them to the steep and rocky area known as the Graves' Caves.

We all dreaded this for several reasons. First, who wants to be around tombs anyway? Not that there really are such things as ghosts, but still, there might be a few ancestor spirits lingering around. You never know.

Second, a *real* for-sure problem was Appius. He was usually lurking somewhere around the tombs, and that guy was dangerous! When he was on a rampage—which was most of the time—he was as strong as ten people.

Sometimes a posse of men would catch him and overpower him. They would force some clothes on him, take him to town, and bind him with chains and ropes.

He might stay there a day or two, regaining his strength after the struggles and beatings he'd been through. Then the demons would take over again, and with fresh power he'd break loose from the chains and ropes and run howling back to the tombs.

A third reason for staying away from the Graves' Caves was that the pigs didn't much care for the steep and rugged hillside in that area. They didn't feel at home there. After all, they're pigs, not mountain goats.

Yet we had to go to the tomb area with our two hundred pigs in spite of these problems and our dread of the place. Soon we could tell that Appius was hanging around nearby. Sometimes we heard a wolflike howl in the distance; sometimes the breeze brought a weird chanting cry to our ears; sometimes a screeching demonic laugh rang out across the hills.

Once I even saw Appius. He was prancing naked among the pigs. Then he got down on his hands and knees, pulling up grass and stuffing it in his mouth like they were doing. They just continued grazing and ignored him.

Then in the early afternoon, a sudden storm darkened the sky. From the east a strong wind swept down the hills to the lake, swiftly changing its calm blue surface into mountainous gray peaks. These waves threw themselves fiercely on the rocks below our hill. Jagged streaks of lightning tore through the boiling black clouds, and thunder rolled and reechoed across the hills and the lake.

I only hoped there were no boats out in that furiously raging sea. We fled to the nearest cave to escape the slashing rain. The pigs tried to shelter themselves under some of the scruffy trees clinging to the rocky hillside.

Then even more suddenly than the storm had appeared, it left. The surface of the lake smoothed out, the thunderclouds with their noise and flashing lights scudded off to the west, and the sun was back. Its rays turned the drops of rain clinging to the leaves and blades of grass into diamonds. Glad it was over, we came out of our cave.

"Look!" I cried, pointing down to the lake. "There *was* a boat out in that storm!"

It was a medium-sized fishing boat, coming toward the shore below us. By then it was close enough that I could see there were about a dozen men aboard. They weren't people I knew, but they looked like they might be Jews from the other side of the lake.

Putting in to shore here was unusual. In case I didn't mention it, most of the Jews counted us Greeks to be just about as unclean as pigs and tried to avoid us the same way they avoided pork. But here Jews were. Maybe the storm had just put them off course or damaged their boat, and they needed to land for rest.

Just as they were pulling up, I noticed Appius loping down the hillside, running toward their boat.

"Oh, no! Look!" I called to my friend Stephen. "We'd better warn them!" We raced down the hill as fast as fast as we could, afraid he might kill or injure someone.

Well, Appius got there first. But instead of attacking them, we saw him lie on the ground, stretching himself out face down, as if before an emperor.

I didn't hear what the leader of the group said to him. A man in a white cloak seemed to be in charge. Later someone told me that this man, Jesus, had already commanded the unclean spirit to leave Appius.

However, we all heard his shouted reply. Appius screamed at the top of his voice, "Leave me alone, Jesus, Son of the Most High God! I beg you, don't torment me!"

Jesus asked Appius, "What's your name?"

He roared, "I'm Legion."

We all know there are about six thousand soldiers in a Roman legion. Perhaps he meant he was so filled with demons that they couldn't be counted.

Frankly, I don't understand what happened next. It scared me so much that I still can't recall it without shivering. I can only tell you what I heard and saw. I can't explain it.

As it turned out, this Jesus had power over the demons, power to make them leave Appius, and they knew it. You could hear their shouts coming from Appius, like a hundred different voices speaking at once. "Please, we beg you, don't send us back to the bottomless pit where we came from! Please!"

I guess they knew they had to leave and they didn't

want to go into the deep. Yet they knew they had to go somewhere, so those hundred eerie voices screeched, "Let us go into those pigs over there—send us into them."

"All right—go!" commanded Jesus.

And they did!

Appius fell down, crumpled up like an empty bag. Our pigs gave one great squeal! Then they ran and stumbled and snorted and leaped down the hill and splashed into the lake. They drowned—every one!

It makes me think there must have been at last two hundred of those evil spirits. Think of how much they wrecked—the life of Appius for years, and then our pigs!

Since then I've been puzzling over all this. *What happened to the demons when our pigs drowned?* Did they drown, too? Or did they end up trapped in the bottomless pit after all?

But at that time I wasn't thinking about those things. Stephen and I and the others ran back to town. We were so excited and scared and our story was so unbelievable that I'm sure we didn't make much sense. But we told everyone we met what had happened.

Most of all, we knew that we had to tell our masters. What would Philo do when he knew his pigs were gone? I was responsible for them! Would he beat me? Would I have to spend years and years of working for nothing to pay him back?

Almost the whole town streamed out to see for themselves what had happened, since most of them didn't believe our fantastic story. When we got back to the shore, there sat Appius at Jesus' feet. With clothes on. Calm. In fact, he was calmer than any of the rest of us.

Some of the bodies of the pigs were bouncing on the waves; others were washing up on the beach. It was all too frightening.

The chief town official spoke what everyone was thinking. He asked Jesus and the men with him to leave as quickly as possible. "Please, just go. We don't want you here."

"I'm going, too. I'm going with him," Appius declared. And he turned to Jesus, "You've saved me from evil that filled me and tortured me for years. Let me come with you!"

"No," Jesus replied. "You go home now. Go to your family and your friends and tell them how God has helped you."

So that's what he did. And he's still talking about it.

A year or so later, we heard that Jesus had been put to death, and some even said he had come alive again. Appius believed this and told us, "Jesus is the Son of God. The demons in me knew it. . . . Are we humans less intelligent than they?"

As for Philo and the other pig-owners, after they had helped send Jesus away, they set us herders to work. We gathered up the bodies of the pigs, and then butchers and salters went to work.

Traveling merchants were able to sell most of the meat that way, dried or salted—but as export only. No one from our town wanted to chance eating the meat of those demon-infested pigs.

With the money from the meat sales, the owners were able to buy more young pigs and begin again. But somehow they still blamed us too, so they fired us and hired replacements.

But I didn't care. I no longer had any heart for that work. Now I'm a baker's assistant, and instead of pork, I meditate on crusty loaves and raisin tarts and sweet honey-coated meal cakes.

6

Unclean?

by Janna of Gennesaret

My best friend, Hanna, and I were the same age. Our families lived next to each other, and she and I had known each other for as long as we could remember. We spent as much time together as we could, but I'd hardly ever been in her house. My father, Jairus, didn't allow me to go there, so she came to our house.

Father was a leader of our synagogue, and he tried to be an example to others in his obedience to God's laws. The problem was that Hanna's mother, Naomi, had an illness that made her "unclean." She'd been this way ever since Hanna's birth twelve years before.

It was a difficult birth and something had happened to Hanna's mother. Ever since, she'd had almost continual bleeding—not a great amount, or she would have died before long, but enough to make her tired and weak. She depended on Hanna's help with the daily household chores. But that wasn't the worst. The bleeding meant that she could *never* become "clean."

My father and the other leaders said our law barred her from any participation in our Jewish festivals. She could not attend any synagogue functions. The law states that a woman is unclean until seven days after her monthly flow of blood stops. Well, Naomi never got up to the seven days.

Even worse for Naomi was the fact that anyone who touched her or her bed or her chair was also unclean. So, not only her, but her husband and Hanna too, were unclean.

Naomi had certainly tried everything anyone could suggest for a cure, but she never got any better. She had also pleaded with the synagogue officials that her case was special: God would not want a person to be considered always unclean because of an illness which could not harm anyone else or spread to anyone else.

Finally Naomi had pleaded that her family not be considered unclean, so that they might be allowed to participate in at least some religious ceremonies.

All her pleas were refused.

"We don't excuse the families of those who have leprosy," the synagogue leaders stated. "Your case is no exception. If it's too great a hardship on your family to live the way you do now, you can go and live apart from them, as the lepers do."

Ephraim, Hanna's father, wouldn't hear of that. He became bitter against the religious leaders. My father wasn't a Pharisee, but two of the other synagogue leaders were, and he wasn't able to get them to be any more lenient.

Then two years ago Hanna's father died. Everyone wondered what would happen to her and her mother. How would they be able to live? They couldn't do any laundry or cooking or housework for others when they were always "unclean."

This was so disgusting because they were the cleanest people around. They were always washing and bathing and scrubbing.

Some of the Gentile families of our town, who weren't concerned about our Jewish ideas of "cleanness," let Hanna and Naomi do work for them. Thus they managed to get enough money to live on.

Being friends with Hanna, playing with her, made me unclean too, even if I didn't enter their house. So when I was eleven, my father warned me that I needed to be thinking about giving up my friendship with Hanna.

"You may still be her friend," he assured me. "But when you're twelve, you'll be old enough to participate in the Sabbath rituals and in Passover and Pentecost and our other great religious holidays. You'll have to be ritually pure to do it."

When I became a woman and began to have my monthly flow of blood, like all women I would still be "unclean" about half the time, no matter what I did. I'd be "unclean" during the time of my flow and for the next seven days as well. It didn't seem worth it to give up Hanna just so I could be "clean" half the time. But if Father commanded me to, I'd have to obey.

Not long after my twelfth birthday, I saw a little blood appear. Mother was delighted—her daughter was now a "woman." I passed through my first period of "uncleanness," thinking, *Well, nothing will stop me from seeing Hanna during the time I'm impure. If I'm impure, I can't get more impure!*

A month or so after that I became very sick with what we soon saw was the yellow sickness. I felt so ill that I could eat almost nothing. I just lay in bed, too weak and nauseated to move. My skin turned yellow and my eyes too.

Father found a doctor, who told me not to move. I should just lie still and probably I'd get better. He explained that the yellow color was the evil and sickness inside me leaving my body through my skin— that's what made it turn yellow.

I believed him, because my skin was not only yellow, it began to torture me. I was unbearably itchy everywhere.

Then the scribe from the synagogue, the expert in interpreting God's law, came to see me. He announced that since the sickness was coming out of my body through my skin, it was like a bodily discharge, and therefore I was unclean.

The next days I remember little besides pain and weakness and crying to my father for help. I think I remember saying, "Oh, Daddy, help me—even if I'm unclean, can't you help your Janna?"

Then my sight began to fail. I could hardly see the things around my bed—they were getting dim.

"Mother, where are you?" I moaned.

"I'm here," she comforted me, taking my hand.

"Where's Daddy? I want him too," I gasped.

"He can't come right now. He'll be here soon. He's heard that Jesus is in town. He's the one everyone says has helped many sick people. So Daddy's gone to find him and bring him here. He'll make you feel better. You'll soon . . ."

Mother's voice was fading. I heard no more. I could see only gray; then that turned to black. But I soon saw a light, a small one. It grew bigger as it came nearer to me—or was I approaching it?

Then I saw that there were people standing in the light; they were reaching toward me. I saw Grandma . . . and there was Hanna's father . . . and my great-grandfather, Josiah! But they had all died . . .

"Come, Janna," Grandma greeted me. She looked so happy, not all shrunken and weary, like when she'd been so sick before she died. Oh, yes! I wanted to be with her and be well and happy again, too.

I thought I felt Grandma's arms around me, welcoming me.

* * * * * *

Someone was calling me. I opened my eyes and sat up, helped by a stranger who had hold of my hand. There were three other strange men in the room. Why was everyone looking at me like that?

Mother began to cry and shout at the same time. I got up to go to her—and almost fell over! The stranger took my arm and told Mother, "She needs food now to regain her strength. Go and get her something to eat!"

Mother rushed out of the room, and Father hugged me tightly. Then I realized I felt perfectly well! I guess Father was so excited that he forgot I was still unclean.

"I can never thank you enough," my father was telling the man. Then I remembered what Mother had said about Father searching for a man named Jesus who could make people well.

"Did you make me well?" I asked him. "I was *so*

sick, but now I feel great!"

I looked at him anxiously. "I'm sorry you needed to touch me. I'm still unclean because of my illness."

He just smiled and said this: "People think about the outside of the body. God looks at what's in your heart. Uncleanness—and cleanness—they both come from within you.

"Your friend's mother is well now, too. Ask your father about it."

I didn't realize at the time what Jesus was saying or wonder how he could know who my friend and her mother were. In fact, I hardly heard him because of all the noise outside.

What a racket! Why, it sounded like the weeping and wailing the hired mourners put on when someone's died. And I heard flutes piping too, like when Grandma died . . . Grandma—my dream . . .

"Go to the window—let them see that you're all right now," Jesus directed me. "But don't tell them what happened."

"You mean—that weeping and wailing is for me? Do they think I died? Did I die? I had a strange dream, and Grandma was there . . ."

Jesus didn't really answer me. He only added, "Those mourners out there said you were dead. But I told them you were sleeping!"

I went to the window and waved. One of my aunts and a neighbor lady fainted right on the spot—or acted like they did. Perhaps they were put out that they had torn their clothes and pulled down their hair and used up some of their best wails for nothing!

* * * * * *

I've told you now what I know firsthand. Later I received secondhand reports from my mother, my father, Naomi, and Hanna.

Father had found Jesus in the center of town. It was a mob scene, but he was desperate and forced his way through the crowd. He went down on his knees before Jesus and begged him to come with him because he was afraid I was dying.

Jesus agreed to come, and they were trying to hurry along through the pushing and shoving crowd. All at once Jesus stopped and exclaimed, "Who touched me?"

No one answered except Peter (one of Jesus' followers who was in my room when I "awoke"). He dared to speak what the others were thinking: "Master, the crowds are pressing in against you.

Jesus insisted, "Someone touched me for healing. I felt some power leave me."

It turned out to be *Naomi!* Hanna had helped her mother struggle through the mob, to get near Jesus. Finally Naomi was close enough to reach out and touch the edge of his cloak.

When Jesus asked who touched him, she stood and flung her headcloth back from her face. She was afraid, but she spoke, even though her voice trembled.

"I'm Naomi. You all know me—and fear me—because of my twelve-year illness. I so desperately wanted to be healed! I touched his cloak—and I've been healed! I feel well for the first time in . . . so long!" And she bowed down at Jesus' feet.

He declared, "You're well, my daughter, because of your faith. Go in peace."

My father was happy for her, and to see her healed

encouraged his faith, but he was anxious for me because of the delay.

Before they could be on their way again, our servant Hiram arrived and told Father, "Janna has died. You don't need to bother the teacher any longer."

Jesus heard him and assured Father, "Don't be afraid. Believe, like Naomi did, and your daughter will be saved."

By the time they and the crowd arrived at our house, there was another swarm of people, the professional mourners, already surrounding the place.

The news that I'd died had spread quickly and the mourners had already begun their ritual. Before entering our house with his three companions and my father, Jesus made a statement to the curiosity-seekers who'd followed him there, and to the weepers and wailers: "Don't weep; she's not dead. She's sleeping."

But they laughed at him—before they began to weep once more.

He came into my room, took my hand, and called me back.

I came back! Praise God!

7

It Was a Miracle

by Jason of Bethsaida

I hurried into the house. "Mom, may I go? Please! Everyone else is going!"

She smiled tiredly. "I don't know, Jason. Go where? Why? You'll have to calm down and explain a little."

"Why, go see Jesus and his disciples. Abe and the other guys have been wanting to go and hear him talk, to see if he really heals people. Abe said he's bound to come to Bethsaida one of these days. Well, today's the day. Abe saw their boat putting in just south from here.

"He was pretty sure it was them, and now he's seen people coming from over Capernaum way and the villages around there—an awful lot of people. If we don't hurry, there'll be too many people, and I won't get to see him! Please, Mom!"

Even though I didn't mention the most important reason I wanted to go, I think she knew.

"Of course you can go. I wish I could, too. But if you'll take Benny along, that would be a big help to me, and maybe I'll be able to get a little rest."

My excitement died down. Benny's my four-year-old brother. He's okay, but I didn't really want him tagging along. Oh, well. Mom had been very tired since my baby sister was born a month and a half ago.

My father was a trader who traveled to Tyre, transporting dried fish and oil from the olives of Galilee—and anything else left from produce sold locally. In Tyre these products were sold and shipped all over the Empire.

Because of his work, Father was away from home most of the time. This made it difficult for Mother when she didn't feel well. So I really shouldn't mind helping out by taking Benny.

"How long do you think you'll be gone? Will you just be here in town?" she asked.

"I don't know how long, but I think we'll be out in the hills. Everyone was headed that direction."

"I hope it won't be too far for Benny. And you. You'd better take along something for a snack." She slipped into a leather pouch the extra flat barley breads left from breakfast plus a few dried fish. I poured water into a small skin, dipping it from the water jar I'd filled for her yesterday.

Benny begged, "I wanna help carry. Give me something." Both the pouch and skin were about equal in weight, but I gave him the skin since it was smaller and he could put its strap over his shoulder.

"Come on, Ben, let's go," I called out.

"C'mon, Jason, let's go," he replied. He always tried to say and do everything I said or did.

The streets were full of people, all going toward the hills northeast of town. Well, at least we wouldn't be the last ones. That is, if Benny's little legs didn't give out. And with my crooked foot and crutch, I wasn't much better than he was when it came to walking.

It wasn't a holiday or anything, but you'd have thought it was. Everyone who was self-employed or who could skip out from work seemed to be part of the exodus. Lots of kids too. No one would be at synagogue school today.

Before we were even out of town, Benny was asking, "Are we gonna have our picnic-snack now? I'm hungry."

"No, we're not." But I stopped and gave him a drink of water.

It was nice to get out in the country. The rainy season was just ending, and the hills were green and grassy and dotted with wild flowers of all colors. Benny wanted to stop and pick some for Mom, but I persuaded him to keep moving by promising that we'd get some for her on the way back.

I didn't see my friends in the crowd. I supposed they were too far ahead by now. Maybe I'd find them after we got there.

When we came to the top of a hill, people ahead of us stopped moving forward. I could see Jesus sitting at the bottom of the hill facing us.

Some of the people began sitting down around Jesus and then began filling the hillside facing him. Others were milling around, trying to decide where would be the best spot to sit so they could watch and listen.

I wanted to get as close as possible. I hoped to hear what he said, but even more I hoped he could fix my leg.

When I was six, I fell from a tree I was climbing and broke my leg. I still remember how painful that broken bone was. It slowly healed but didn't grow together straight. Now my right foot sticks out at an angle, making that leg shorter than the left one.

I usually hopped along with the help of my crutch. Sometimes in the house, I'd lurch around without it, using walls and furniture to steady myself. I could only watch most of the fun and games of the other boys, but I'd pretend I was part of the group by keeping score and by refereeing their disputes.

I pushed politely through the crowd, trying to head downhill toward Jesus. People did squeeze together to let Benny and me get closer. Perhaps they saw my crutch and crooked leg and hoped they might see one of the wonderful cures they'd heard about. We finally found a place near the front.

This was the biggest crowd I'd ever seen. I hoped they'd settle down. Now they were like an impatient audience noisily waiting in the amphitheater for the entertainers to begin performing.

When Jesus began speaking, they quieted down. His voice carried well. Jesus didn't shout, but he spoke firmly, and those who wanted to hear could hear.

To be sure, there was always some coming and going, folks chatting with their neighbors, others waving to an acquaintance on the opposite side of the crowd, and restless children continually on the move. But no one was unruly or making loud noises.

People had heard enough about Jesus so that they wanted to see for themselves—did he really do great deeds of power, curing the sick? Did he really talk against the religious leaders whose heaps of rules made life nearly impossible?

Did Jesus really say the strange things people said he did? "No more an eye for an eye. When someone injures you, don't fight back. Instead, love your enemies."

While listening, even I could figure out that his teachings *were* different from what I'd learned about our traditions in the synagogue school from the rabbi. It differed from what we were told in Sabbath service by those who commented on the Scriptures. Most of the people were smiling as they listened, but others raised their eyebrows and glanced at each other.

With each thing he taught us, Jesus had a little story, which was easy to remember and repeat to others. I'll tell you a few things I remember best from his words.

"Don't be a judge of other people. You'll be judged the same way you judge. If you judge harshly, you'll be judged harshly."

"What do you mean?" someone called. "Why, I know my neighbor's a thief..."

"Be careful. Look at yourself first. Or else you'll be like a man who has a log in his eye! Instead of taking care of that problem, he's all concerned about his neighbor who has a speck of dust in his eye!"

Everyone burst out laughing.

Jesus continued, "Take the log out of your own eye

first. Then you'll see clearly to help your neighbor with his speck of dust.

"Don't love only your friends but your enemies as well. Then you'll be children of your heavenly Father. He sends his sun and his rain on everyone, doesn't he? The good and the bad alike.

"If you love only those who love you, or if you're friendly only to your friends, you're no better than anyone else. You won't receive any reward for that. Even the Gentiles and the tax collectors, whom you despise, do that much. Be like your heavenly Father, who loves everyone.

"Be generous. Give, but without making a show of it. Hypocrites like to have trumpet players marching ahead of them in the streets to announce their gifts. Don't be like them. They have already received their only reward—being seen by others. They'll have no reward from God.

"Instead, do your giving secretly. God knows, and he'll reward you. He'll give you back at least what you gave. The grain bag you emptied in order to give to others, God will heap full and overflowing.

"You've heard my words. If you act on them, you'll be like the wise man who laid the foundations of his house on the rock. Strong winds, torrential rains, and even floods beat against the house. But it stood firm!

"Yes, you've heard my words. If you *don't* act on them, you'll be like the foolish man who built his house on the sand. Strong winds, torrential rains, and even floods beat against his house. It fell and was swept away!"

As the day went on, I occasionally took Benny for a little walk so he wouldn't be too restless. Actually, he was good and listened at least part of the time. Then all at once, he piped up with his high child's voice, "I like that man. I like his stories!"

Jesus smiled at Benny and beckoned for him to come forward.

Benny, usually bashful, ran to him. Jesus held him awhile, and then taught the crowd, "You need to become like a child to be part of God's kingdom. Children are trusting. We should depend on our heavenly Father the same way a child depends on parents."

Benny didn't really understand all that. He had something else on his mind. He pulled on Jesus' tunic to get his attention. "That's my big brother, Jason," he said, pointing to me. "Can you fix his leg? Then he could walk better."

So far Jesus had only been *talking* to us. Now he looked at me and directed, "Come here, Jason."

I limped over, and he told me to sit down. His hands were feeling my leg as he asked me what had happened to it.

While I explained, he placed his hands firmly around the spot where the bone had grown together wrong. That part of my leg began to get warm, and it felt like the bone inside was softening and becoming bendable.

Jesus' hands pressed, and I saw my foot changing position—it was becoming straight, in line with my leg! When he removed his hands, I could see that my right leg was just as straight as my left. The warmth faded away, and I knew that the bone was no longer pliable but strong and firm.

Benny clapped his hands, "You did it, Jesus!" he shouted, and gave him a kiss.

"Oh, thank you!" I exclaimed. "I'll never forget what you did. And I won't forget what you taught us, either. I want to *do* what you teach, like the wise man."

Then I looked around and saw that behind me there was a line of other people who hoped for healing, too. So I took Ben and walked—just like everyone else walks!—and returned to our spot. Some of my friends had seen from a distance what had happened and now came to see up close.

"Wow, Jason! That's incredible!" exclaimed Abe.

Thomas declared, "I get first choice! I want you to be on my team!"

I wished I had something to give to Jesus, to show how thankful I was, but I had nothing. Then I realized I was hungry, and that reminded me of our lunch. It wasn't much, but Jesus would be glad for *something* to eat after talking to us for so long and then using up his strength and energy to heal sick people. He looked tired.

I opened the pouch and took out the smallest bread and the smallest fish for Benny. Then I walked—without limping or pain!—to the nearest of Jesus' disciples and offered him the five loaves and two fish that were left.

"This isn't much," I admitted, "but please, I want Jesus to have it. He must be tired and hungry after all he's done."

"Thanks, Jason," he said as he accepted the food. "I'm Andrew. Yes, Jesus will need this. We came here to relax and to get away from people, but it hasn't worked out that way."

Just then Jesus' helpers gathered around him, and I heard one of them say, "Master, it's late afternoon, and we're out here in this isolated place.

"You'd better send the people away before it gets dark. Then they can go to the nearest villages to buy some food. And those who are too far away from their homes to get there by dusk can find places to stay overnight."

Jesus directed, "You give them something to eat before they go."

One of them protested, "We didn't bring along anything to eat, even for ourselves! We thought we were going to be here alone and could buy what we needed at some village."

"Even two months' wages wouldn't buy enough for everyone to have a small piece of bread, and we don't have that kind of money, anyhow," added another.

Andrew spoke up. "Master, we do have a little something. Jason brought us his own lunch to give you for healing him. There are five barley loaves and two fish—maybe enough for you and one other person."

"Bring them here to me," he instructed. "Do you remember what I said? What will happen to those who are generous? Tell the people to sit down. Arrange them in groups of fifty."

One woman near me was listening in. "You did a good thing to give up your own lunch," she told me.

"Come on, Lois and Martha," she recruited women near her. "You too, Esther and Joanna and Dorcas. We're all from the next village. Let's get what we had left there for our families' suppers. We can bring it to Jesus and his disciples to eat." And off they went.

The people thought that was it for the day, and they were getting ready to wander off to the villages for food and lodging or to start for home. But now the disciples were asking them to sit down again. Jesus himself was helping to organize things and called out to the people to sit down and have something to eat before they left.

So I sat down too. I sure wondered what the plan was. There were a lot of hungry people, each one puzzled as to what would happen.

Because of the way we were being grouped, it was easy to estimate the size of the crowd. I looked around, counted the groups, and did a little multiplying. Finally I decided that in just the men's groups there were at least five thousand people.

There weren't as many women and children. It's harder for them to get away, like my mother, for instance. But I'd say there were two or three thousand mothers and children, too.

Just when everyone was seated, the women I'd seen hurry off returned, all six of them. Each one was carrying two baskets of food. They could have easily sold what they brought to the first people they met, but they gave it all to Jesus.

"Master, we want to share with you, too, what we have. There should be at least enough for you and your disciples."

Jesus thanked them. Then he took my loaves and fish in his hands, and looked up to heaven. He prayed, "Father in heaven, thank you for these generous gifts and for those who have given their own food to share with others. Bless this food so it may bring honor to your name."

Then he broke the loaves and broke the fish and passed the pieces to the disciples and continued by breaking and passing what the women had brought.

I could see—we all could see—what happened. But as for understanding! I know that some (those not present) have claimed that when the people there saw how a few had shared, others brought out their own food hidden in their bags and pouches. They claim that's how everyone had food to eat.

It's true that some (like my mother) had thought ahead and brought along some bread or olives or fish or cheese. Now they brought out their food and ate. But it was more, much more than that.

I watched when Andrew came to my group of fifty with half a loaf in his hand. He broke it and gave half to the first person. Then he broke the rest in half, but what should have been a fourth was as big as a half, and each time he broke and gave half of it, the half loaf was still as large as it had been at first.

How could this be? Well, how could my leg be straight? How could blind people see again? I don't know, except that it was God's power working through Jesus.

What Andrew was doing, all the other disciples were also doing as they went from group to group. We thousands of people ate and ate, as much as we wanted. What Jesus had said was true: "God will give back what you gave. The grain bag you emptied in order to give will be heaped full and overflowing."

I saw it proved for myself and again for the women. When everyone had eaten as much as they wanted, Jesus gave the women's baskets to the disciples and had them gather up what was left over. There was so much left that when the women got back their baskets to take home to their families, they were loaded with more food than they had brought!

Jesus used the bread to explain himself to the crowd: "This bread has strengthened our physical bodies. You remember how God sent manna from heaven for the physical bodies of our ancestors. But now God has sent the true bread from heaven to give life to the whole world. *I am the bread of life.*"

Then he sent us away. Those last words of his echoed around in my head. They were too mysterious for me to understand. But he said them, so I believe them. I know he gave from his life into my life.

8

I Hated Myself
by Rufus of Caesarea Philippi

I hated myself—so much that I wanted to die. I think my father knew that. Why else did he make sure that the slave Philibus was with me at all times? Philibus helped me when I had an attack and kept me from harming myself. I hated him for helping me.

I hated my father, too. If he really loved me, as he said, why didn't he know the best way to show it? Just let that possessing spirit succeed in throwing me into the water or into the fire and end it all!

I hated the gods for creating such a creature as me. They refused to listen to my father's pleas to cure his son. They ignored the rich offerings he brought to their priests for my healing.

I'd been this way for as long as I could remember. At first I didn't realize it, though. That was before I began hating. At that time, I only knew that Philibus was always with me. I knew that sometimes I would wake up in my bed and it was evening. Yet the last thing I could remember was playing with my dog in the courtyard in the afternoon.

Philibus would say, "Your spirit went away, Master Rufus, and I carried you here so you could rest."

Then one day when I was seven or eight years old, I went with my father to the stalls in the marketplace where the goldsmiths work. He wanted to have some earrings made for my mother.

The whole market area was crowded and busy as usual: people were selling vegetables and fruits—cucumbers, melons, grapes, onions. Others were marketing clay pots or meat or live sheep and goats. There were piles of multicolored yarn for weaving and cloth already woven; or a choice of little statues of the gods and goddesses. You could find anything you might need or want.

Suddenly a scream pierced the hubbub of market noises, and people scattered in fear. There in the middle was a girl, lying on the ground. Her body was stiff and shaking all over. Her eyes turned up in her head. Horrible sounds came from her mouth, and saliva poured out like foam.

A woman, seeming to be her mother, was weeping and trying to hold the girl's hands so she wouldn't claw herself and tear her skin. The people watching—those who hadn't run away—were raising their right hands, making the five-finger sign to ward off the evil eye.

"What's the matter with her?" I asked my father. "She looks and sounds so awful. Is she dying?"

At first he didn't answer. Finally he said, "She's not dying. She's sick though, with the seizure sickness.

Some people think evil spirits enter a person and make them like that. Others think, like I do, that it's a mysterious illness sent by the gods.

"Watch her. After awhile the seizure will leave, and she'll be all right. She won't remember anything that happened. And then maybe after a day or so, or after a week or a month, it will happen again. We never know when it'll happen."

"But, Dad, how do you know so much about it? Do you know that girl?"

Again he hesitated. Then he confided, "No, I don't know her. But I do know someone who has an illness something like hers. That's how I know what will happen. After awhile she'll wake up and be right again."

"Let's go!" I exclaimed. "I don't want to see her anymore. I don't like her."

"I think we should wait," he insisted gently. "Your mother and I have known that we must tell you some time. Perhaps now is the time. I'm not sure."

He looked troubled but he went on. "You know how Philibus is always with you—you complain about it often enough! You've noticed too that we don't let you play much with other children or take you out very often, although today I did. It's because . . . because *you* have the seizure sickness, too."

"What?"

"Those times when you wake up and don't remember what happened? Well, you've had a seizure or a convulsion, something like this girl's."

"No! No!" I shouted. "Not like that! I'm not like that! I won't be like that! I can't be!"

Then the air around me began to crackle and spin. The next thing I knew, I was lying on the floor of the goldsmith's booth, my father and Philibus beside me. Slowly I remembered the girl. I remembered my father's words.

"Is it true? Did I . . . did I act now like that girl did?"

"Well, yes, something like that. It wasn't a long attack. I think you'll soon be feeling all right, and we'll go home."

"Did people see me? Did they stare at me too—like they did at that girl?"

"Yes."

After that for a long time I refused to leave the house. My tutor continued to come there to teach me as before. Sometimes my parents would invite my cousins or neighbors to come for visits. I was sure they knew about my horrible illness. I was convinced they were afraid of me and tried not to get too close to me, and that their politeness to me was only an act.

Because of the way they treated me (or the way I thought they treated me), I became more and more feared and disliked. I was touchy and aggressive and obnoxious.

When my cousin Julia tried to talk to me, I made fun of her long nose and how she played the lute. I insulted my neighbor Hermes. I said he was a sissy because he was interested in history and art. He had friends and I didn't, so I was jealous of them and mocked them.

I was the same with all the young people my parents could persuade to try to be friendly to me. I hated myself, and so I hated everyone else, too. I wanted to avoid everyone because I feared and dreaded that they would sometime see me in one of my "fits."

Now that I knew about my problem, I found that I could sometimes tell when an attack was coming. But I could do nothing to prevent it. I would have that crackling and spinning sensation, and my head felt like it would burst.

Afterward I felt incredibly tired and sleepy. I began to make Philibus tell me each time how long I had been unconscious and everything I had done.

It became evident to my parents and to Philibus and me that the attacks were coming more often, lasting longer, and becoming more violent. Instead of lying convulsed on the ground, I sometimes had great strength and tried to destroy myself by escaping from Philibus and throwing myself on the cooking fire. Or I would flee to the river and attempt to jump in to drown myself.

My hatred spread from myself to others. I even tried to harm my parents and my keeper; they were preventing me from doing what I wanted to do—end my life.

Then one day I overheard my parents talking. "Can't we do anything else?" my mother asked. "He's getting worse."

"I know," replied Father. "At first it was only the illness, the seizure sickness. Now it seems as though there's also an evil spirit in him."

"I've heard some talk about a healer," Mother continued. "He's been going around among the Jews in Galilee. But apparently he's done some cures among the Gentiles as well.

"I heard of one healing over near Tyre—a woman whose daughter was cured of an evil spirit. Phoebe told me. She learned about it from her mother, whose friend is an aunt of this girl. Some of what that girl went through sounds like what happens with Rufus. Her mother found this Jesus and begged his help, and now her daughter is perfectly well!"

"You know how these rumors spread," responded Father. "You can discount at least three-fourths of what you hear. Still, I'm willing to try anything. A Jewish charlatan is probably no worse than any other kind. Where would we find this man? I can't picture Rufus willingly going anywhere, let alone on a long journey."

"That's just it! This healer has just been seen in our area. He and his followers passed through here. Phoebe heard this from Lois. They've gone north to make a pilgrimage to Mount Hermon, and a crowd is gathering in the foothills, hoping to see them when they return."

"All right. I'm desperate enough to try anything. We'll go there and wait with the others. If Philibus and I can't handle him, I'll hire some other fellows to help us get him there. We'll camp there till this healer appears."

At first I was angry about the idea. But when I saw that my father was determined, I decided for once not to make too great a fuss. I was bored and ready to get away from our house and our town. By then I was feeling stuck with my illness, feeling that "whatever will be, will be."

So what if I got a convulsion along the way or among strangers? Let them be scared good and proper, as I'd been when I saw my first—that girl in the market. Perhaps deep down I even had a small spark of hope that this man could make me well.

I didn't mind the walking—it was good for me for a

change. Always ahead of us loomed Mount Hermon and its coldly beautiful snow-covered peaks.

After about a day's journey, we came upon a collection of all sorts of people. Some had tents and had been there several days already. Some had only their cloaks to wrap themselves in at night. Philibus inquired and found that this was the right place. All these people were hoping to see Jesus.

Philibus also learned that the teacher and three of his friends had left for the summit two days before and should return the next day. But he had left nine of his followers here at the bottom to wait for the four climbers.

The report was going around that these nine men also had some healing powers granted to them by their master. They were heard bragging that they had done a good bit of healing down in Galilee, and now here they were also doing some cures. So far it had been fairly minor things, people said: some festering boils healed, some fevers lowered, and some near-sighted eyes strengthened.

"Well, let's try," declared Father. "I'm not particular. If his helpers can do it, we won't need to wait till the master returns."

We found the group of disciples—apprentices, I suppose you could call them. My father began to explain my case. Then, so I'm told, I put on a spectacular demonstration to illustrate what he was saying.

The disciples tried to send the evil spirit out of me, by words and commands and by laying their hands on me. When the convulsion ended, they thought perhaps they had succeeded. But in less than half an hour, I was seized again, worse than before.

By midmorning the next day, we saw four men descending the path toward the waiting crowd. My father didn't hesitate. He ran up to them and called, "Teacher, I beg you to look at my son, my only child. He has the seizure sickness, and a spirit seizes him—it shrieks and convulses him until he foams at the mouth. It's destroying him! I begged your disciples for help, but they could do nothing!"

I was hanging back, but Jesus saw me. He not only looked *at* me, he looked right *inside* me. Then he looked at his disciples and the other people standing round, a look both angry and sad.

Finally he exclaimed, "What people! You're faithless and perverse! How much longer do I have to stay among you and put up with you? Bring the boy here."

Then as Philibus led me closer, the whirling and crackling began again, and I fell convulsed before the whole crowd. I know from my father what happened then.

Jesus asked Father how long this had been happening to me.

"Since he was a small boy," he answered. "The sickness and evil spirit are destroying him. If you can—please help us!"

"If you can!" repeated Jesus. "Everything can be done—if you believe."

"I want to believe!" exclaimed my father. "Help me to truly believe."

Then Jesus commanded the evil spirit to come out of me, that spirit of hatred, and he cured me of the seizure sickness, too.

They say I lay there like I was dead for awhile. When I regained consciousness, it seemed like any other time I awakened from a spell—I was very tired. But then I noticed a difference. I was different inside. There was no hatred any more. I had feelings of joy and peace and love—feelings so foreign to me I could hardly recognize them at first.

I think my father and Philibus realized right away that I was well because I smiled at them, something I hadn't done for a long time. So we knew the evil spirit had gone. For awhile I had a dread that the seizure sickness might return, but it never did.

Jesus and his disciples were ready to move on by the time I was fully recovered and had strength enough to get up and walk. We found him as they were about to leave. Father was very grateful and wanted to give some money to the healer.

Jesus wouldn't accept it and encouraged him, "Continue to believe, and your faith will continue to grow. God's kingdom is here now for everyone."

"But we're not Jews, as you can tell," Father reminded him.

"God's kingdom is here now—for everyone. It makes no difference, though I myself was born as a Jew and have ministered first to the Jews. Our Scriptures teach God's love for all—but we haven't always understood this."

As we were leaving, a man came after us. "I'm Judas," he said in a low tone, "one of Jesus' twelve disciples. I'm the treasurer for the group—I take care of our purse and purchase our food and other things we need.

"Jesus isn't too interested in these practical details, and he doesn't realize how much it takes to feed us all. He doesn't know how low our balance is right now. So I'd be glad to accept, on behalf of the group, the gift you wanted to give."

Father looked a bit surprised, but responded, "Yes, of course," and gave him a generous amount. After that, we went on our way.

From then on we tried to keep track of Jesus. We heard several reports that certain ideas, such as those he'd shared with us, helped to get him into trouble with the Jewish leaders and led to his death.

We probably weren't as surprised as some when we heard that Judas was dishonest in his job as treasurer, and that it was he who sold Jesus to his enemies.

We have come to believe the rest of the things we heard about Jesus, too—that he was raised from death, and that he is the way into God's kingdom.

9

The Light That Became Darkness
by Korah of Chorazin

My father is well known in our town. He's an expert in our laws and traditions—a scribe, who teaches and applies the Law of Moses to daily life. Besides that, his zeal in following these laws and traditions have made him Chorazin's leading Pharisee. I'm proud of the standing this brings our family.

Yet sometimes I resent being forced to conform to all the rules in the smallest details, so that everyone can see that I, his son, reflect his piety. I resent being on display. Though I'm receiving the same training as he received, I'm not as sure as he is of the rightness of the Pharisees' way.

In recent times the activities and teachings of this traveling unofficial rabbi, Jesus, have become a concern to my father. It's the main topic of conversation whenever he and the other teachers of the Pharisees get together.

I've listened to them when they meet in our house. Every time they have something new to complain about. Sometimes it's another incident of how Jesus broke the Sabbath by healing someone. Or they complain that he told someone he forgave their sins—which only God can do.

They admit that he drives out demons, but they claim he does that with Satan's help. And they're really upset over how he's been so friendly with unclean people, such as tax collectors and sinners.

Yet when some of the lower-class people discuss Jesus, I overhear things altogether different. They talk about the same problems and questions, but from them I hear Jesus' side and the answers he gives.

He says the Sabbath is for our benefit, not to make our lives difficult. So, on the Sabbath it's all right to do good things, such as healing. He healed a paralyzed man whose sins he said he'd forgiven, in order to prove that he had the right to forgive.

He claims that Satan cannot be divided and chase out Satan, so how could he drive out demons with Satan's help? And he explains that he's friendly to the unclean and sinners because they are the ones in need, not the righteous.

I thought I'd like to see and hear this fellow for myself. So far my father had done neither—he'd only listened to reports of others. I wasn't sure why. Was he afraid that he might find out he was wrong? He doesn't ever like to admit he's wrong. But who does?

Then the day came when Jesus was actually in our

town. Now there was no excuse for not going to hear him ourselves. My father was still reluctant. He said, "Going to hear him only makes him seem more important than he really is."

"He must be pretty important, as often as you and your friends discuss him," I suggested. "All you know now is only hearsay, secondhand information."

"I know we need to go," Father admitted. "At least then we'll be sure someone is there who can contradict what he says when he presents false teachings."

As it turned out, he wouldn't have needed to worry about that!

We found Jesus in the marketplace talking to the people. The crowd I saw around him wasn't what I had expected.

Instead of lots of common people, there were mainly Pharisees and their scribes—recognizable by their haughty looks, extra-long fringes on their robes, and large phylacteries or Scripture boxes tied on their foreheads and arms. These Pharisees were mostly strangers to us.

"Where are they all from, Dad?" I asked. "Do you know any of them?"

"I know a few. I see some from Capernaum and Gennesaret, Bethsaida too. But I think most of them look like they come all the way from Jerusalem. I'm surprised. They must be even more concerned about his false teaching than I realized."

Jesus could see who his audience was. Maybe he had come up against some of these characters before. I wouldn't have been surprised if some of them were following him around to stir up opposition everywhere he went. Most of them looked grim and stern.

What Jesus was saying wasn't the kind of things I'd heard about before. People had been repeating what he'd said: "Do good to those who hate you" or "Ask God and he'll give to you, just like you give good things to your children when they ask you."

Today, to this testy audience, Jesus was speaking forcefully and almost bluntly.

One Pharisaic scribe asked Jesus, "What sign can you perform to prove you have the right to do and say all these things?"

Jesus' eyes were blazing, as though he had enough of their criticism and was going on the offensive. "This is an evil generation. You want a sign? You'll receive no sign—except one that has already been given—Jonah.

"He was a sign to the people of Nineveh. They repented when they heard Jonah's preaching. The people of Nineveh will condemn you at the judgment because you have someone greater than Jonah here, but you refuse to repent!

"The Queen of the South came from afar to hear Solomon's wisdom. She also will condemn you at the judgment because you have someone greater than Solomon here, but you refuse to listen."

How did Jesus dare to speak like that to these scribes of the Pharisees? He was telling us that *Gentiles* would be more favored by God at the day of judgment than us Jews! That the Gentile sinners from Nineveh and the Gentile Queen of the South listened and repented, but we wouldn't!

Jesus also seemed to claim that he was greater than Jonah or Solomon!

I could see that the temperatures and tempers of

the Pharisees were rising. Their grimness and sternness were changing to anger.

One of the strangers came up to my father. "Someone told me you're the leader here in town. We'd like to get Jesus away from his simple admirers and followers and really question him. We'd appreciate it if you could invite him—and us as well—for a meal. That way we'll be able to pin him down more easily than we can here in public."

Father didn't look too happy, but he agreed to do it.

Meanwhile, Jesus wasn't through with his criticisms. "Your eyes are your body's lamps. If your eyes are healthy, your body is full of light. If they're not healthy, your body is full of darkness. Think it over. Has the light in you become darkness?"

I puzzled to understand his words. Did he mean that the light was the faith and way of life God had given us, but that we had turned it into darkness? Could it be true that, instead of being a welcoming beacon to draw others, we had become a black pit?

My father stepped up then and invited him to our home. He accepted, so Father sent me off to alert Mother that Jesus and a bunch of visiting scribes and Pharisees would be coming to lunch.

We have some capable servants and a large house. So, even though it was a rush, everything was arranged by the time they arrived an hour later.

The water jars were at the doorway for the ceremonial washings we Pharisees strictly carry out. The tables and couches were arranged in the shaded courtyard. On the tables were the cucumbers marinated in vinegar and oil, and the bread for the first course, along with the goblets and wine.

To get things off to a bad start, Jesus bypassed the water jars, omitting the ceremonial water-cleansing, and sat down at the table. The others all solemnly dipped their fingers and raised them to let the water run to their wrists, then lowered their hands to let the water run off.

No one said anything out loud, but I saw plenty of raised eyebrows and heard some muttered comments: "I told you so. What did you expect from a carpenter?"

Jesus knew, though, what people were thinking and whispering, and he didn't hesitate to respond.

"You Pharisees are careful to clean your cups and dishes—on the outside. But inside you're full of greed and wickedness. The one who made the outside made the inside too, didn't he? If you really want to be clean, get rid of that greed and wickedness, rather than dipping your hands in water!"

They were too stunned and furious to reply. But Jesus hadn't finished. He'd just begun!

"Woe to you, Pharisees, you hypocrites! You're proud that you give a tenth of everything, even to the smallest herb. But you neglect God's justice and love! Practice justice and love! And that doesn't mean you should neglect the tithing!

"Woe to you, Pharisees! You're like the blind leading the blind! You love attention, so you take the best seats in the synagogues. You want everyone to notice you when you parade through the marketplaces. How sad!

"You're like unmarked graves on which people walk without realizing they're tramping over the bones of the dead."

Finally a Pharisaic scribe spoke up. "When you talk like that, you're insulting all of us!"

"Yes, you're included too!" Jesus answered. "Woe to you, scribes, hypocrites! With all the rules you add to the Law of Moses, you load people down with burdens too hard to bear. And you won't use one finger to help them. How sad!

"You pay to build memorial tombs for the prophets your ancestors killed—they killed them, and you build the tombs!

"Woe to you, scribes! You had the key to knowledge, but you didn't enter. Then you not only took away the key, but you kept those who wanted to enter from going in."

He was surely wrong. Wasn't he? He must be! Why didn't one of these wise teachers stand up and prove he was wrong?

Jesus was the one who stood up then. His eyes seemed sad and yet somehow caring as he looked at each of the hate-filled faces and left.

The rest of the dinner party didn't discuss whether there might have been any truth in his accusations or whether there might be any possible means of improving our ways of doing things. The discussion concerned only how to catch Jesus saying something they could use to bring charges of blasphemy against him.

I couldn't help but partly agree with what Jesus said. If only he had been less harsh, more tactful. Still, their minds had been made up before he spoke to them in that confronting way. Perhaps he'd hoped to jar their self-satisfaction. If so, it didn't work.

I wouldn't be surprised if he knew then that he was on his way to a dismal end, that there would be no turning back.

Some of the men at the table with him that day were among those of our top court, the Sanhedrin. Later they met in Jerusalem and helped sentence Jesus to death.

10

Up a Tree
by Jerusha of Jericho

We had a lovely house, built in the Roman style and located along the main road leading out of town. A row of cypress and sycamore trees shaded it in front.

Inside, giving coolness to the central courtyard, were mimosa and palm trees. The courtyard was tiled with mosaics except for the pool in the middle where golden carp darted and flicked their tails.

I had my own room off the courtyard, and in it was a chestful of finely woven and embroidered robes and mantles, some even made of silk. I was unlike most girls in that my father provided a tutor to educate me. I could speak and write Greek and Latin and Hebrew.

My parents loved me (and my four younger brothers and sisters) and satisfied all our needs and wants that they could. *Could* is the important word. What they couldn't do was to make others love or accept us.

Because of my father's work, our fellow Jews hated and despised us. So did the Greeks and Romans of Jericho. Father was the chief tax collector for the Romans in the provinces of Galilee and Judea.

The Jews regarded tax collectors as being traitors to the Jewish nation because they worked for the hated Romans, foreigners ruling our land. They felt that we had denied God as well, and they considered us to be unclean sinners.

The religious leaders could not bar us from going to the synagogue, for even interested Gentiles could attend. But we no longer went because of the unpleasant, spiteful words and looks of the people. They turned their backs on us and shook the dust from their clothes and shoes at us.

We got their message: We want nothing more to do with lowlife like you.

Yet at home we still observed the Sabbath, and we read the books of Moses and the prophets. But we didn't interest ourselves in the traditions and interpretations of those extra rules given by Ezra and later teachers.

The Gentiles despised my father, too. No one likes to be forced to pay the customs and duties which my father's assistants collected. The government had a contract with my father. He would pass on to the rulers a certain amount of tax money from the people each year. Anything he gathered beyond that was profit for him and his assistants.

Under this system, anyone unscrupulous could make people pay unfair amounts and then keep all the extra money. We weren't poor by any means, as you can tell from what I've already said. Yet my father tried (and usually succeeded) to do his work fairly as well as profitably.

Father regarded his work as necessary and thought it was unjust that he and his family should be outcasts of society. People even called him names like Shameful Shorty, Tiny the Traitor, Rip-off Rascal, or Zap-'em Zack. Not to his face, though. They were afraid he would increase their taxes if he knew. But he knew, all right.

Soon I would reach the age of marrying. I was resigned to it being difficult for my family to find me a suitable husband. About the only place for them to look would be among the families of other tax collectors or those who were collaborating with the Romans.

Most of the other tax collectors and collaborators did tend to be rather sleazy and crooked. When I tell you this, I know I risk sounding like the people I've been criticizing!

Now I'll get to the events I want to tell you about. A while back something strange had happened to one of Father's assistant tax collectors. Matthew Levi had the franchise in Capernaum. He suddenly quit in order to join some new teacher or preacher who was traveling around Galilee.

It was midyear when he resigned, so he gave Father all the money he'd collected during the first six months. He sold other assets he had so he could pay what he owed for the rest of the year.

It was a sudden decision with no warning, but later he stopped off at Jericho while this teacher and his followers were en route to Jerusalem, to give an explanation to Father.

He was still quite excited about his new life. "Jesus is a great teacher!" he exclaimed. "Everywhere he goes, hundreds and sometimes thousands of people follow him. He has a new interpretation of the laws and traditions.

"To Jesus, people such as tax collectors *aren't* unclean—at least not more than others. We do need to make changes in our lives, like everybody else does, in order to follow God as we should. Jesus even calls God 'our heavenly Father.'

"Why, he had no hesitation in coming into my home. I invited all the other 'sinners' and outcasts of the town who were willing to enter my 'unclean' house. I had a big dinner party, with Jesus as the guest of honor.

"You can imagine how excited the Pharisees and others were when they saw Jesus eating and having a good time with all of us 'sinners'! He just told the critics, 'It's the sick people who need a doctor, not those who are well! I haven't come to talk to the righteous about repentance, but to the sinners.'

"And Jesus doesn't say paying and collecting taxes is wrong. He says we should give to Caesar what belongs to Caesar, and to God what belongs to God."

"And exactly what does that mean?" asked Father "That could be interpreted several ways!"

"Well, I think he means we should pay our respect and our taxes to Caesar. And to God we owe our highest allegiance and our lifelong love."

I didn't realize at the time what a big impression Matthew's words had made on my father, but apparently he often thought about this Jesus and his teachings. He also tried to pick up other information about Jesus from whatever sources he could.

Father is normally a rather quiet person. He's forceful and tenacious—but in a calm way. So we'd seldom seen him as excited as he was when he got word that Jesus would be passing through Jericho on the way to Jerusalem. He was determined to see for himself who Jesus was. He thought this shouldn't be difficult to do, since his tax office was right along the main route through the city.

The rest of us were interested, too, but I had my own idea of a good spot to wait to see Jesus. It was a comfortable shady place with an excellent view of the road. So I took sister Sara (who's eight) and brother Jonathan (ten) and a snack of grapes and bread. We went outside our house and up one of the sycamore trees along the road.

Even though I had outgrown tree-climbing, I hadn't forgotten how. Soon we were nicely installed. This was much better than standing in the sun and perhaps not being able to see because of being crowded out by taller people. Jonathan and Sara were still small, but so was I. Even though I'm as tall as my father, that isn't very tall.

We sat there, talking and munching our snack. After awhile we could hear the noise of many people. Looking toward the central city, we could see a throng moving along. It was progressing slowly because the people were packed so tightly together. Then from a narrow back alley to the left of the route, someone dashed out, running ahead of the crowd.

"It's Father!" Jonathan cried.

"Here, Daddy! Come here!" called Sara.

He arrived, and we reached down to help him climb up. He was breathless for a minute, then gasped,

"I just couldn't see a thing there in town. There were too many people. I could tell they were heading this way and thought of the tree you kids sometimes climb. I'm sure I looked silly, a grown man running like that and climbing a tree—but I don't care. I must see Jesus."

Now the crowd burst from the narrow street and spread out, advancing faster in our direction. In the middle I recognized Matthew and then could easily pick out which one was Jesus. "He must be the tall one there, near Matthew," I guessed.

"Yes, yes," replied Father. "He's talking to them as they walk along. I wish I could hear. They say he's a great storyteller."

"Maybe we'll overhear a little if they pass close enough," I said eagerly.

But the crowd was too noisy for us to hear, even though they were coming right to our row of trees. Suddenly the crowd stopped moving because Jesus had paused. There he was, standing just beside our tree and looking up! He saw us!

I was so embarrassed at first. Then I thought, *He's smiling. He doesn't care. Maybe he's glad we wanted to see him so much that we climbed up here!*

Matthew was whispering something to Jesus. Then Jesus spoke, still looking up at us. "Zacchaeus, hurry and come down! I'd like to stay at your house today!"

Father was so pleased and excited he nearly fell out of the tree by trying to slide down too quickly. When he reached the bottom branch, Jesus gave him a hand.

Father bowed and responded, "Please, Lord, we

would be very happy to welcome you and your disciples to our home. We would be greatly honored."

As they were entering the gate, Father turned and called to the crowd, "Anyone else who wants to enter my home to hear the Lord speak is invited as well."

The others weren't about to enter such an impure building as a chief tax collector's home. They stood there, scowling. When we kids clambered down, we got some black looks from those still in the street. Many of them did more than frown.

One called out, "Ha, what kind of a teacher is that—gone into the house of that cheating traitor!"

Another snorted, "I'm glad to know what kind of a person he really is—willing to be—no, *asking* to be the guest of a notorious sinner!"

Jonathan called out, "Sinner yourself, Simon! You drink too much wine, and you beat your slaves!"

I hurried him and Sara inside before Jonathan could say anything more. But I was glad he'd spoken up, and I heard a few snickers from some of the bystanders who knew Simon and his ways.

Mother and the servants soon had a feast prepared for the occasion: roast veal; rice spiced with cinnamon and cumin; a salad of tomatoes, onions, and black olives; flat bread and yeast bread and pocket bread; three kinds of cooled melons (red, yellow, and green); and honey wafers. Father permitted us children to eat near the others so we could hear and see Jesus, too.

Jesus told us many things about God, our loving heavenly Parent. He explained the Scriptures in a way that made sense. Though we could tell that Jesus loved us rather than despising us, he didn't overlook our sins.

He helped us to see that it wasn't only hypocrites and Pharisees who were far from God; so were we. We didn't live as we should. He explained this with stories. I'll tell you only one of them—a very short one.

"If you have a hundred sheep and one becomes lost, don't you leave the ninety-nine and go out searching for the one that's lost? You search until you find it. Then you put it on your shoulders and rejoice all the way home.

"At once you call all your friends and neighbors together and say, 'Come and celebrate with me! I've found my lost sheep!' So, I tell you, there will be more joy in heaven over one sinner who repents than over ninety-nine so-called righteous persons who think they don't need to repent."

Father was absorbing every word Jesus said, like a thirsty man gulping down water offered to him. When Jesus stopped speaking, Father stood up. Everyone looked at him, and a crowd of critics was even watching and listening through the open windows.

He declared, "I want to be a true follower of the heavenly Father. I have much more than I need, so, Lord, I'll give half of my possessions to the poor. If I've cheated anyone, I'll pay them back four times as much."

When I heard this, I was so proud of my dad!

In response, Jesus announced in a loud voice, "Today forgiveness has come to this house. Zacchaeus is as much a child of Abraham as anyone else in Jericho. The Son of Man came to find and to save the lost."

At the end of the dinner, we sang a psalm together in celebration of God saving people like us. Then Jesus and his disciples went on their way, up to Jerusalem.

From this incident some people decided that my father had been very dishonest. Yet simple mathematics shows that isn't true. If so, he couldn't have given away half his possessions and also repaid people four times their overpayments. If he had cheated a lot, we would not only have been penniless, but deeply in debt.

Our life has been different, though, since that day. Has it been better? That may be debatable. I'll explain, and you can decide.

For one thing, we moved to a much smaller house and began eating only simple, everyday food. We were satisfied to see some of the poor benefit from the gifts Father gave them. He didn't just scatter money around but tried to help those in debt get out from under their heavy loads. He helped others purchase what was necessary to set up small businesses.

As to repaying the few he'd defrauded, that led to more problems. When others saw what he was doing, many tried to claim that they'd been defrauded as well. It became a big mess. What should he do if one of his assistants had cheated someone? Was my father responsible for that?

Some of Father's assistants became angry at having their methods of collecting taxes questioned. They began to hate Father for trying to change the system and to make them be honest, simply because he was determined to be honest himself.

Father finally needed to give up his job. Now he is trying to support the family by dealing in dates. He upgraded the small grove of date palms he'd inherited from his father, and we are working together to make a business by selling not only our own dates but those of the other growers.

As for our relations with most other people—they aren't any better. Followers of Jesus' teachings aren't popular in Jericho. Most people, even though they had despised Father, had thought he was a sharp businessman. Now they laugh at him.

We do have a few new friends—some who had also been outcasts but now are followers of Jesus. Others whom Jesus healed also visit with us. Bartimaeus, who had been blind, is the best known of these, but there are others as well.

Together, we make a small group of people who are trying to learn more about Jesus and to follow his teachings. We often gather in our modest central courtyard to pray and praise God for saving us through Jesus. From this group comes my beloved fiancé, Justus.

We know how Jesus was killed and we believe in his resurrection. Matthew visits us occasionally to help and encourage us and to bring news of the Jesus believers in Jerusalem and other places.

We often talk about that day when Jesus visited our house. It's our special family story. Our lives were changed, and now we know that God loves us.

11

The King?
by Baruch of Bethphage

I loved to sit by our gate and just watch the people walk by. In less than a week, it would be Passover, the biggest celebration of the year, and many pilgrims were already arriving. If they were coming from the north or the east, they passed by Bethphage and our gate on their way up to Jerusalem.

What my dad and I (and everyone else) were really curious about was whether Jesus would show up for the festivities this year. Just a few months ago he had been in the area—in Bethany, the village next to ours. That's when he did his greatest and most dangerous miracle. He brought Lazarus back to life—a man who'd been dead for four days!

I know some people don't believe he did it. But we know Lazarus. We attended his funeral feast! Like everyone else, we were skeptical when we heard that he'd been brought back to life. Like everyone else, we went to see if it was true. And I assure you, it was.

He wouldn't talk about anything he'd seen or done "on the other side." He'd only repeat: "It's truly me before you. I know I was dead. I know that I'm now alive and that Jesus did it. But that's all I have to say."

The ones with plenty more to say were our religious leaders. Instead of this event convincing them that Jesus was our Messiah-King, it made them more determined than ever in their plotting against him. He threatened their power. Rumor said they wanted to get rid of Lazarus as well. That's what I mean by saying it was a dangerous miracle.

Now the question on everyone's mind was what Jesus would do. Would he come to Jerusalem? Or would he stay in Galilee or Perea until things calmed down a bit here?

"What do you think, Don? Will he come?" I patted the nose of our young donkey as he looked down at me. We had him tied by the gate.

"It's time we give that young fellow some training," declared Dad. "He's old enough now to start doing some hauling."

"I think he might be good for riding," I responded. "But today wouldn't be a good day to start working with him. There's too much traffic on the road."

"You're right about too much traffic today. But as for riding, I think he's too skittish. He doesn't even like to be touched by anyone but you."

It was getting hotter, and the shade was shrinking as the sun rose higher, so I went inside for a drink of water. When I got back, two men were untying Don!

My father protested. "What are you doing? That's

my colt you're untying!"

One of them answered, "The Lord needs it. He'll send it back later."

Then I recognized them as being two of the group who went everywhere with Jesus. I'd seen them several times at the home of Lazarus or on the way to or from Bethany where he lived.

Dad asked, "Does he want to ride it? It's not trained yet, and it has never been ridden."

"I'm not sure, but I think so."

"Well, for him, you can take it. We were wondering whether you fellows would be here for the festival. It may be dangerous for you. Some people are really riled up. Baruch, you'd better go along in case you're needed to help handle the donkey."

I was willing and ready for a little excitement. Until now I'd only seen Jesus from a distance.

As we traveled, I was surprised how docile Don acted, walking right along with the men and causing no problem. We soon came to where Jesus and the rest of his band were waiting. Quite a crowd was forming around them.

All the strange people and noise seemed to have no effect on Don. I continued to be surprised at him. He stood calmly as some of the men laid their cloaks on his back and then helped Jesus to mount.

Then one of the disciples called out a verse from the prophet Zechariah:

> Look! Your king is coming to you,
>   Humble and mounted on a donkey!

He pointed to Jesus and shouted, "Here he is! Our king!"

Then everyone began to cry out:

Hosanna!
Blessed is the king who comes
 in the name of the Lord!
Peace in heaven,
 and glory in the highest heaven!

Some of them threw down their cloaks, and the donkey began climbing up the Mount of Olives toward Jerusalem, walking on a carpet of garments. Some of the people hurried back to pick up their cloaks from behind the donkey and ran ahead to place them again in front of Jesus.

Meanwhile others quickly pulled or hacked leafy branches from palms and other nearby trees. They waved them and sang:

Blessed is the king who comes
 in the name of the Lord!

Some bowed and laid their branches on the road before the king. Again and again the refrain echoed through the hills:

Blessed is one who comes
 in the name of the Lord—
the king of Israel!

As we moved along, more and more people kept joining the throng. We'd reached the top of the Mount of Olives now and were descending into the valley of the Kidron Brook.

Then we'd have a last ascent to enter Jerusalem, the city of the king. The temple gleamed white and gold above us, beckoning us on.

Some people were nearly delirious with joy. *What will he do?* I wondered. *Will he call down fire on the Romans? Will he send a plague to strike down those plotting against him?*

Not everyone was carried away like I was. There were also a few Pharisees in the crowd, and I heard them call out to him, "Teacher, tell your disciples to stop making such a pitiful spectacle of themselves! Shut them up!"

But Jesus replied, "If they were silent, these stones would shout out!"

Then his mood abruptly changed as he gazed at the city towering above us. He began to weep, and I heard him say, "O Jerusalem, if you had only recognized today the things that make for peace! But your eyes are closed. Your enemies will crush you. They will not leave one stone upon another because you would not recognize that God was visiting you."

What did he mean? We didn't want to hear such things, and so we continued our demonstration for the Messiah-King. We went all the way to the very temple itself.

By then most of the people with us had scattered. They had arrived in Jerusalem, the goal of their pilgrimage.

Some of us kids followed Jesus on into the Court of the Gentiles. Don was tied outside. But inside, what fun we had! The temple courts were crowded.

There we saw money changers—thieves, really, because they cheat out-of-towners who don't know the exchange rates. They displayed old coins from Tyre that did not carry Caesar's image. People had to buy them to have money the priests would accept for offerings to the temple.

Other merchants were selling animals and doves for worshipers to sacrifice, but they overcharged badly.

The animals were protesting, stirring up dust, and leaving droppings. What a mess! It looked like a market instead of a temple.

Jesus shouted above the noise, "The Scripture says, 'My house shall be called a house of prayer for all the nations.' But you've turned it into a den of robbers! This is the court of the Gentiles, but there's no room for them to come and worship God."

Then Jesus turned over the money changers' tables and chairs. With a whip made of cords, he began to drive out the sheep and the oxen. We kids joined in and helped chase the animals, swishing our palm branches at their vanishing rears. It was almost a stampede toward the entrance.

The money changers—what a riot! They were dashing about and scrambling all over the place, trying to grab their rolling coins before anyone could help themselves.

When all the traders and their animals had left and things were calming down, we kids who still had palm branches waved them above our heads and sang, "Praise to the Son of David!"

The temple officials were really ticked off by then. They had been making a bundle of profit with their cut from the temple commerce which had just left. But Jesus was so popular with the people that they were afraid to do more than complain.

"Don't you hear what those brats are saying?" the temple leaders asked him.

"Yes," replied Jesus. "Doesn't it remind you of Psalm 8?

> Out of the mouths of children, O Lord,
> you have prepared praise for yourself."

Then suddenly, everything was over. Jesus and his disciples left quietly for Bethany to spend the night with Lazarus and his sisters. I trailed along behind them part of the way, leading Don home.

I felt let down and disappointed. After the thrill of the parade and the excitement of clearing out the temple—nothing!

Well, I thought, *maybe tomorrow he'll take over and do his king thing.*

He never did do what we expected. Everything went downhill from there. The entry into Jerusalem had been on the first day of the week—by the night after the fifth day he was arrested. And on the sixth day he was executed. His enemies had triumphed.

Now many say and believe that he came back to life and is a king, but not the kind of ruler we were waiting for. They teach that his kingdom means serving God and that anyone can be a part of it. I don't know what to think.

I do know that Don has developed into a model beast of burden. He certainly is not a war horse, like most kings would ride. So it makes sense when people say Jesus is a different kind of king. If he really is alive, perhaps he is the prince of peace expected by Isaiah.

12

The Plotting Priests
by Jeruba of Jerusalem

I'm a doorkeeper at the palace of the high priest. My job is to check all visitors—their identities and the reasons for their visits—before the guards let them pass into the palace.

The priests think that we Jewish slaves should be grateful for the privilege of serving them. What a joke!

Annas and his five sons (all former high priests) and his son-in-law, Caiaphas (the present high priest), are seven of a kind—proud, sly, cruel, and caring nothing for the people. They're rich schemers who rake in their wealth from their businesses of buying and selling animals in the temple and from the money changing that goes on there.

They'll do anything to keep firm control of their power and influence. This you'll see from the events that I'm going to recount.

Being so wealthy, they could well afford paid servants to staff and run this mansion. But they're too stingy and greedy, so they prefer slaves. And all of us slaves are Jews. They think they're too holy to defile themselves by using Gentile slaves.

My family became their slaves in my grandfather's day because of a sheep plague. It killed most of the flock of sheep he was raising for the high priest, Annas, to sell in the temple. Annas said we were responsible to pay for all the dead sheep. When we couldn't do so immediately, our family became slaves of the high priest's family.

This happened before my birth—so I haven't personally known what it's like to be free. But my parents remember, and they've taught us what our religion says about slaves. We know that according to Jewish law, if Jews become slaves to other Jews, they are not to be slaves forever, but are to be freed after six years.

Don't the priests know the Scriptures? Or do they purposely disobey them? I know how *I'd* answer that question.

The high priests' palace is an unhappy place to work and live. Among the slaves, just as among other people, there are always disagreements and rivalry and power struggles. There are spies and traitors among us, too.

You might think that slaves would be among the first to at least secretly support those working toward throwing off the Romans and those they appointed—our masters, the high priests. But no! We had to be very careful of everything we said, especially when Malchus was around.

Malchus was the only one of us with the prospect

of becoming free. We all knew that if he could supply enough information, true or false, about any rebel ideas circulating among the slaves, freedom would be his reward.

For some time we'd been aware of the activities of a certain Jesus from Galilee. People were saying he was a great healer and teacher. Some claimed he was the Messiah, or one of the old prophets returned to life. We didn't pay much attention at first. But when my brother Titus, personal slave and aide to Caiaphas, began reporting to us how upset the priests were becoming, we paid attention.

The priests had begun to send spies and agitators among Jesus and his followers, hoping to catch him saying or doing something against either our Jewish religious law or against Roman civil law. They even were trying to entice him into some mistake, anything to find an excuse to arrest him.

He had attracted so much attention and enthusiasm that the priests were getting worried about their hold over the people. Worried enough that they had begun plotting and planning together with their enemies, the Pharisees and their scribes! How weird!

I knew something unusual was up when I received instructions to let certain scribes and Pharisees enter the palace. We knew that before, they could only come in with special permission. Later Titus told us the purpose of these unusual visitors—to plot together with the priests against Jesus.

Then it was Passover week, and the whole city was in an uproar. Jesus had staged a grand entry into Jerusalem with thousands of his shouting and singing followers. He was courageous or foolhardy enough to go to the temple courts, chase out the animals for sacrifice, and rebuke the sellers and money changers!

That evening there was laughter and rejoicing in these slave quarters (discreetly, of course), but seething fury in the priestly halls.

It was my week to be on duty at the gate in the late afternoon through the first watches of the night. What daytime that I didn't need for sleeping, I could use as I wished. So the morning after this temple incident, I decided to go there myself and see what could be seen. I might even get a glimpse of Jesus.

The outer courts weren't completely free of commerce, because some merchants were starting to return, but it certainly wasn't as crowded or as noisy or as smelly as it usually had been.

As I walked by the columned archways of Solomon's Porch where rabbis and their students often sat for their discussions, my heart gave a leap! Somehow I was sure that the one sitting there was Jesus. He was under an arch with a large crowd gathered around him.

Those nearest to him, I took to be his twelve disciples. Their simple clothing and manners made them easy to distinguish from the richly dressed, smooth-talking, sophisticated Jerusalem scribes and priests, who were also crowding around on the outside.

One disciple I recognized. He was a cousin of one of the high priests and had been to the palace several times. I also especially noticed two of the others. Later I saw them both again at the palace while I was at work.

One was dark-haired and handsome, but with a sulky, dissatisfied look, as though frustrated by the way his teacher did things. The other was a big, strong, vigorous man, watching Jesus closely with a proud and excited air.

However, the intensity of Jesus himself drew me nearer. His eyes seemed to pull us into his thoughts and heart. Everyone was affected by his forceful words and his air of authority. Those with open hearts and minds felt attracted to him, as to a magnet. But others were repelled.

A few other girls and women were in the crowd, so I relaxed, knowing I wouldn't be noticed. I stayed long enough to observe the following incident. A group of opponents began to question Jesus. I recognized some of these chief priests and scribes because they were among those I'd seen enter the palace recently.

"Tell us," their spokesman demanded, "who gave you the authority to do what you do, especially what you did yesterday in the temple?"

Oh, no! If Jesus said he had God's authority, that he was the Messiah, they would have him arrested! If they let him go and the Romans heard that the Jews had a king, that would be terrible trouble for all of us. The Romans claimed *Caesar* was our only king.

Jesus replied, "I have a question for you. If you answer mine, I'll answer yours. Was the work of John the Baptizer from heaven, or was it of human origin?"

They had no answer ready and began discussing among themselves in low voices. I was close enough to hear snatches of their conversation.

"If we say 'from heaven,' he'll say, 'Why didn't you believe him then?' . . . Yes, and then we'd have to recognize Jesus' authority because John called him the Messiah. . . . But we daren't say 'of human origin'—the people are so convinced that John was a prophet. . . .

Right—they'd be ready to kill us if we said that. . . ."

Jesus and all the rest of us were waiting for their answer. Finally their spokesman muttered, "We don't know where John's baptism came from."

That brought hoots and laughs from the onlookers. Remarks were flying such as "Ha! You're our religious experts and you don't know? . . . Cowards! Afraid to give your opinion!"

Jesus closed the matter. "Then neither will I tell you by what authority I am doing these things."

What could they say then? I left feeling pleased at the way he could handle their trick questions and accusations. Yet I was also afraid that perhaps he didn't realize how determined they were to trap him. Did he know that they wouldn't hesitate to use foul means if fair means failed to stop him?

Soon after that I learned that Jesus' actions had had another result. His enemies were going to do more than try to trap him in public. I got word from the chief steward that a group of scribes, some chief priests, plus the captains of the priestly and temple guards—all these were to be quickly and quietly admitted that night.

Later Titus told me, "Sister, it's getting worse for Jesus. The result of this secret meeting was the decision that Jesus *must* be arrested and put to death by any means possible, and as soon as possible."

Late the next afternoon, a man came to the gate, demanding entrance. He wanted to see the leading priests or the high priest. I recognized him as being one of Jesus' twelve disciples—the dark, handsome, discontented one.

"Please state your name and the reason for your request," I insisted.

"I'm Judas Iscariot. Priest Obed knows who I am. Tell him I'm ready to discuss the matter we talked about earlier. I assure you, they'll want to see me."

I sent a guard with the message. He was back almost immediately with Priest Obed, who welcomed Judas warmly and led him directly toward the reception chamber of the high priest.

Before long, Judas reappeared. His face was blank and told me nothing. A disciple of Jesus in conference with the plotting priests? I tried to imagine what this event could mean and could hardly wait to ask Titus.

Later Titus told me he'd been attending Caiaphas as usual when this Judas was ushered in and greeted with much friendliness and honor. The man had either been a spy and never a true follower of Jesus—or else he had been a true follower but had turned against Jesus.

Judas had come to "sell" his master. "I know your plots and your desires," he said. "You'll never catch him the way you're going about it. He's too clever, and the people are still for him. I know his habits and can lead you to him when there's no crowd around—at night and in private. How much are you willing to pay?"

The deal was made for thirty pieces of silver.

The priests told me then that I was to admit Judas at once whenever he came. The next night, he was at the door again, excited. He rushed in and was taken immediately to Caiaphas, even though it was late.

They must have preplanned carefully for this time, because it wasn't long until a posse was ready. It was composed of temple police and palace guards with clubs, and a few Roman soldiers armed with swords.

Some slaves were carrying torches and lanterns. And a few priests and scribes were along to oversee the operation.

All together, they nearly filled the courtyard. The swords glinted in the light from the torches and the courtyard fire, and the clubs were dark and menacing.

Priest Obed quieted the group, then spoke to them.

"At last we're going to be able to catch this rebel blasphemer, Jesus. He's left the city to go to one of the gardens on the Mount of Olives. With him are only about ten of his closest followers. According to Judas here, they'll be mostly timid, tired, and unarmed.

"Judas will lead us to the garden. The one he greets is the one you're to seize. Never mind about the others—but Jesus mustn't escape. Now let's go."

They passed through the gate, now open wide. I wished I could have locked them in.

My mind considered different scenes. Maybe Jesus would have left the garden before the soldiers arrived. Maybe—if Jesus was the Messiah—he'd perform a miracle against his enemies. Maybe they knew of Judas's betrayal and would surprise the posse by putting up a battle.

None of my "maybes" came true. The armed band returned, one prisoner in their midst, his hands bound behind him. The men were subdued and quiet compared to the jostling, noisy gang they'd been when leaving. My eyes raked the group—Judas wasn't among them. Where had he disappeared to?

Several of them hustled Jesus into the audience room. There a group of leading priests and (past and present) high priests were waiting with some scribes and elders who had been summoned that night.

The other soldiers and slaves flung themselves down for a rest, either lying wrapped in their cloaks or crouched around the courtyard fire to get warm.

Our informer slave, Malchus, seemed to have lost his usual arrogant and superior air and his usual talkativeness. He just sat there and stared into the flames. Then at the same time, he shook his head and exclaimed, "He healed me! Jesus healed me!"

Those of us nearby looked at him in surprise. Another slave, who'd also been part of the band confirmed this report. "Yep—I saw it. One of those friends of Jesus was going to put up a fight. He pulled a sword, and Malchus, who was the nearest to him, had his ear whacked right off! Jesus put it back on! Look—you can't even see where it was cut!"

"He healed me," Malchus repeated, "and he told the one who attacked me, 'Put your sword away. Everyone who uses the sword will die by the sword.' What could he have meant?"

I was called back to my post by the guards and left Malchus there, still muttering. Someone was knocking when I arrived. The guard opened the gate, and I looked out. It was one of Jesus' disciples, the one who was a cousin of the high priest. He came in cautiously, looking worried and frightened.

"This is where they've brought him, isn't it? We tried to follow at a distance without being noticed. I'm afraid, but I've got to know what's happening. Oh, and my friend Peter should be here soon. Let him in when he comes." He passed quietly around the courtyard under its shadowed arches toward the audience room.

Then came another knock. A man was standing in

the shadows and a voice murmured, "I'm John's friend. May I come in?"

"John's gone to see if he can find out what's happening in the audience room," I responded, leading him into the courtyard. "You can wait here, if you like, by the fire."

Then, with the help of the fire, I got a better look at him. "You're one of Jesus' disciples, aren't you? You were with him!"

Instantly he denied it. "No! I'm not. I don't know him. I don't even know what you're talking about!"

Well, he's afraid to admit it, I thought, walking back to the gate. Actually, he probably had reason to be afraid. At least he was brave enough to come and wait among those who had just captured his master.

A little later I went back to warm myself at the fire. I saw one of the other servants near Peter pointing to him. She said loudly enough for everyone to hear, "This man's one of them—he was with Jesus of Nazareth."

"Who, me?" protested Peter. "I don't know the man you're talking about."

Sometime later I went back once more to the fire because it was really cold that night. One of the slaves was saying to Peter, "I know you're a Galilean. I can tell by your accent. You must be one of them. In fact, I think you were in the garden with him! Maybe you're the one who cut off the ear of my cousin Malchus!"

Peter shouted, "I swear to you, I don't know *what* you're talking about! And I don't know *who* you're talking about either!"

Then at the same time, three things happened (connected to one another, though I didn't have any way of knowing it at the time). First, in the silence that followed Peter's outburst came the sound of a rooster crowing in the deep darkness just before dawn.

Second, Jesus was led from the audience room onto the portico to go to another chamber. As he passed by the courtyard, his glance fastened on Peter in a way that showed he had heard Peter's words of denial.

Third, Peter burst into tears and turned and fled from the palace.

I didn't witness what happened inside those palace rooms that night. But I heard that Jesus told them he was the Messiah, God's Son. That by itself was not enough to condemn him. There have been others claiming to be messiahs, before and since.

What really finished him off was his claim that his accusers would see him as the Son of man seated at the right hand of Power (meaning God). They, the top judges of Israel, would see Jesus coming on the clouds of heaven as judge of them all!

That was all the high priest could take. He tore his robes and called it blasphemy. Some there hit Jesus, slapped him, and spit on him. They decided he must be condemned to death.

This group gathered together at night couldn't legally decide anything. But in the morning they brought their recommendation of death for blasphemy to the official court of seventy, the Sanhedrin. This court's "yes" vote condemned Jesus.

However, they had no authority to carry out a death penalty. So they sent Jesus to Pilate, the Roman governor, for a second trial, condemnation, and sentencing. The sentence, carried out that very day, was death by crucifixion.

* * * * * *

I saw Peter again several months later. He and John were brought to the palace by a band of guards, many of the same ones who had arrested Jesus.

They arrested Peter and John because they were preaching that Jesus was alive—and because people by the thousands believed them and were baptized. Now Peter was different. He was bold and brave and willing to tell anyone that he was Jesus' disciple.

The arrest was also because of a great miracle Peter had performed, one that the priests couldn't deny. A man, lame from birth, had lain begging every day at the temple gate—for nearly forty years. This cripple had been healed by Peter in Jesus' name. There he was, well and standing before the council!

With some weak threats, the council released them. Now it was the priests who were afraid to do anything more, because of the people.

My contact with Jesus while he was on earth was short and impersonal. Yet I have learned to know him more now by believing in him and by being one of his followers. We often meet in the temple courts and in homes to praise God and to learn from the leading disciples of Jesus, now called apostles.

13

The Second Thief
by Joanna of Anathoth

I'm not sure when I first began to suspect that my father was a thief. Like most children, I didn't pay much attention to what my father did for a living. I thought he was a trader and that was why he was so often away from home.

I knew that none of the other children liked me, except Hulda, but I didn't know why. She was a year or two older than I, and my only friend.

Then one day when I was walking alone, carrying my water jar from the well to our house, some of the village children began to throw stones at me, shouting,

Thief! Thief!
Your dad's a thief!

I was so shocked that I nearly dropped my jar, but

I shouted back, "Stop it, you horrid liars!"

But they only threw more stones and chanted:

Thief! Thief!
> Your dad's a thief.
> > He'll come to grief!
> He's a crim-in-nal.
> > He'll roast in hell!
> > > And you as well!

Suddenly Hulda appeared. She gave them a threatening look, and scolded, "I see who you are, all of you. I know your names. If you ever tease Joanna again, I'll let our fathers know about it—and that'll be the end of you!"

They turned pale, dropped their stones, and ran for home.

"That's the only way to shut them up," she told me. "Scare them good and proper."

"Thanks, Hulda. You really did scare them. But it won't last. Of course, they were lying, but they'll realize you were lying, too. Won't they?"

"Jo, you're such a head-in-the-sand ostrich sometimes! Maybe I exaggerated a bit, but I wasn't lying. If you're really that ignorant about the situation, ask your dad!" Then she tossed her head and strolled on home.

I was busy as usual taking care of our house and my younger brother, Marcus. He was eight years old, and I was ten. Our mother had died when he was born. But I still had time to think, and I began to feel nearly sick with worry. Father came home three days later.

My father never talked much, and there was silence as we sat on the mat eating the meal of bread and lentil soup that I'd prepared. Finally I couldn't stand it. I blurted out, "Did you have a good trip, Father?"

Then I couldn't stop myself. I heard my voice going on, "Where did you go? What did you trade? Was Hulda's father with you?"

I couldn't stop the tears I felt starting to trickle down my cheeks. "Uh, we'll talk about it later, Annie," he muttered, glancing toward Marcus.

Now Marcus was staring at us both, his eyes wide open. "You mean what the kids say is true? You and Hassen rob and kill people on the Jericho road?"

Now I was staring in astonishment at my little brother. Father sat several minutes with his head bowed in his hands. Then he straightened up. "I guess I knew you'd find out eventually, but I kept putting it off.... I want to explain.

"I *was* a trader, but I'd bought the donkeys, carts, and my first consignment of goods on credit from Jason the merchant. I was doing pretty well, and I'd begun to pay my debts. Then bandits attacked my little caravan and stole everything. Jason said I'd have to pay him back in the time agreed on, regardless of the circumstances, or he'd take us as slaves. I didn't have enough money to do it.

"The next day Hassen told me about his band of robbers and asked me to join them. I had tried everywhere to find work and was desperate, because time was running out, so I agreed.

"Since then, I've found out it was all a put-up job. Hassen's gang robbed me, but Jason was really the brains behind it all. He not only got what money I had to partly repay him for the goods—he also got all the things stolen from me. By now he's probably resold and restolen them several times."

"But Dad, can't you—?" asked Marcus and I together.

"No," replied Father sadly. "I can't get out of it. There's no way. I've helped in robberies, so I'm under a death sentence. If I made any move to leave the group, I'd be turned in to the soldiers—and Hassen and Jason would be rewarded for doing it.

"So now you know. I'm sorry, so sorry." He began to sob, and we cried with him as we hugged him.

* * * * * *

That was four years ago. Our unhappy life went on. I had no friends, not even Hulda. I couldn't forgive her for what her father had done to mine.

We had enough money for food but nothing extra. Father was so much under the power of that gang that he didn't even get his fair share of what was stolen. The bandits made his life miserable because he always tried to avoid taking part in the violence and killing which sometimes were part of the holdups.

Their main area of work was along the winding, mountainous road between Jerusalem and Jericho. In fourteen miles, it steeply descended 3,600 feet on the way to Jericho. It passed through desolate wilderness. Everywhere jutted rocky crags which concealed countless secret hiding places. Five miles from Jericho, a narrow pass on the lonely mountain road was their favorite spot to ambush travelers.

That country seemed to be made for bandits.

Even when people traveled with armed escorts, the outlaws were more often successful than not. Such escorts only signaled to the thieves that this was a group with something worth stealing.

As the eagle flies, our village wasn't far from this road. But only goats and thieves could find their way along the nearly invisible rocky paths and trails that wound through the mountains between the two.

Then it happened—what I'd always dreaded and feared. Hulda came with the news one evening. She had heard it from Hamed, her fiancé and part of the gang.

"Our fathers have both been captured by Roman soldiers! They were being led toward Jerusalem when Hamed last saw them. There's not much chance for them—caught in the act by soldiers. If your father would have fought, perhaps . . ."

"If it weren't for *your* father," I interrupted, "mine would never have been involved in the first place. I know how your father and Jason schemed to trap him!"

We glared at each other.

"I'm going to Jerusalem," I declared.

"What do you expect to do there?"

"Nothing, I suppose. But I can be near him and let him know that I love him."

I didn't know that Marcus had come in till I heard him say, "I'll go too, Sis."

Early the next morning, before the sun had risen, we took the few coins we still had from the last Father had given us and left our village. We did not know when or if we might return.

We went on the track through the hills, heading

west of town to where it joined the route going south to Jerusalem, a place I'd never visited. Marcus had been there, though, last year after he turned twelve. A kindly neighbor and distant relative had taken him along so he could celebrate the Passover. Now it was Passover time again, and nearing the end of the week-long celebrations.

Crowds of people were still going toward Jerusalem; everyone but us was in a festive mood. Though my heart was heavy, I couldn't help but notice so many happy and excited people.

In spite of our sadness, I liked drinking in the beauty of the hills, now mostly green with the spring rains. I thrilled at the awesome sight of the great walls of the city now looming ahead of us.

I might not have noticed a certain field on our right as we neared the city walls. But Marcus, puffed up with knowledge from his previous visit, was pointing out the sights.

"Look, Annie. See that hill there? It's called the Place of the Skull—because of the shape, I guess. It's almost round on top, and those caves in its side look like the eye sockets. It's where the Romans kill their criminals and . . ." His voice died away. He looked miserable, and muttered, "I forgot . . ."

I stared at the hill. Even from a distance I could see bones, including several skulls, littering the field. Perhaps another reason for its name.

"And those big posts stuck in the ground? What are they?" I asked.

"Oh, Annie, don't make me say," he answered.

"What are they?" I demanded.

"The Romans kill by crucifixion. They put the

prisoners . . . on those posts. And leave them there till they die."

"How do they fasten them there?"

"I don't know, Annie. I've never seen . . . I never want to, either!"

"Well, want to or not, we might *have* to see." I pinched my lips shut tightly.

My excitement and joy had vanished. Both of us were in tears as we entered the city.

I had never imagined that Jerusalem was so big with so many people. Marcus thought he could find Josiah's house, where they'd stayed when our distant Anathoth relative had brought him to Jerusalem. If we couldn't stay there, perhaps they could somehow help us find lodging. And help us to find out where Father was and what was happening to him.

Josiah's doorkeeper remembered Marcus. "You can come in, but you'll have to wait a bit. Things are in a terrible uproar right now. John's just come and told us that the governor has sentenced the master's cousin, Jesus, to death! The sentence is to be carried out immediately!" Then he ran off.

We had no idea what or who he was talking about, so we waited hesitantly by the door. People were hurrying to and fro. Some were weeping; others looked like they were in despair. Three people were coming toward the door where we were standing—an older woman and two younger men.

"That one's Josiah," Marcus whispered, pointing to the one on the left.

Josiah was saying, "Aunt Mary, please stay here. John will come and tell us . . ."

"No, I must go," she insisted. "I must be there with my son."

"It may even be dangerous for you, since it's come to this," protested Josiah. "To be crucified like a common criminal!"

"Josiah, I'm going with John. What you do is up to you."

"I don't think I could stand it, Aunt. Please don't go. It'll be more than you can bear."

"I *need* to go. I must try to understand. I never thought it would be like this."

Before they could leave, I stepped forward. "Please, we've just arrived from Anathoth. My brother, Marcus, stayed here last Passover. We came because our father's been arrested for robbery, and we're so afraid . . . You said there's to be a crucifixion of someone called Jesus? Do you know—will more than one person be executed?"

The other man spoke. "We know only of Jesus, my master and best friend. But who knows? The Romans may have others they'll punish at the same time. We're going now to the Place of the Skull. You may come along and see. If your father isn't there, you might be able to inquire about him from the soldiers."

Not knowing what else to do, we went along with them toward that horrible spot we had passed less than an hour before. When we arrived near the gate by which we had entered, the street was swarming with people.

I heard the sound of marching feet. An escort of soldiers pushed the crowd back to make room, but I squirmed my way through the pack. Soon I could see past the few people still in front of me.

A man had just passed, with a group of four soldiers encircling and guarding him. His head was bowed and blood was running down from wounds on his back. He was struggling to carry a heavy wooden beam on his shoulder. I couldn't see his face, but I thought it could have been Hassen.

Now another group of soldiers, surrounding a second man, was advancing. Around his neck hung a sign: HANAN OF ANATHOTH. THIEF. It was Father!

"Ai-e-e-e-e!" A great wail burst from my throat, cutting through the noise of the crowd. Father looked toward the sound and saw me. His mouth moved, but I couldn't catch his words. I think he said, "Go home. Go!" He, too, was bloody and was half-carrying and half-dragging a heavy piece of wood.

I felt an arm around me. It was the woman Josiah had called "Aunt Mary." "That was your father?" she asked.

I nodded. I couldn't speak. Suddenly she withdrew her arm, clasped her hands, and fell to her knees, "Lord, have mercy! Lord, have mercy!" she was praying.

A third group of soldiers was passing. The man in the middle this time must be her son, the one they called Jesus. In front of them, a soldier carried a sign similar to my father's but larger. He turned it from side to side so all could see it. On it was written in three languages: JESUS OF NAZARETH, THE KING OF THE JEWS.

King? Whatever did that mean?

His steps were faltering. We could see he had been beaten even more severely than my father and Hassen. Blood dribbled down his face from wounds on his forehead. It looked as though something had pierced him many places there.

With him was another man, clothed and unbeaten so apparently not a prisoner, carrying his piece of wood for him.

"Please," I asked John, "what does his sign mean? And what are those wooden beams?"

"I don't know why Pilate the governor wrote that—perhaps to mock us all. We thought—no, we were *sure,* that Jesus was our promised Messiah, our king." He shook his head sadly, then went on.

"Maybe, even now, he'll do something. He has the power. I've seen him use it a hundred different ways. He could do it. I'm sure he could. But he won't. I've already lost my Messiah. Now must I lose my friend and master, too?"

There were no other prisoners, so we followed the crowd the short distance to the Place of the Skull. John, in his misery, had forgotten my second question, but now I saw the answer.

One after the other, beginning with Jesus, the three men had their arms stretched out the length of their wooden beam. Their arms were held there by iron nails pounded through their hands and into the wood. Ropes bound their shoulders to the crossbars.

I couldn't watch—but I had to. Though Jesus groaned with pain, I heard him say strange words, like a prayer: "Father, forgive them. They don't know what they're doing."

When their turns came to be nailed fast, Father and Hassen screamed in pain and cursed the soldiers. The crossbars were fastened by rope up on poles already standing. Each condemned man was seated on a peg in the pole. Their feet, resting on blocks of wood fixed to the upright pole, were turned sideways and a soldier drove a nail through the heels into the pole.

Horrible!

Over each suffering man, the soldiers nailed the signs they had carried there.

At the time I knew nothing about this cruel punishment. Since then, I've learned a lot! The Romans didn't invent crucifixion but adopted it from other nations. It was used by Persians, Greeks, people of Carthage, Germans, Britons, others, and even by a Sadduceean high priest to crucify some Pharisees a hundred years ago.

The Romans use this beastly form of execution as the penalty for rebellion or tumult or highway robbery. They reserve it for slaves and non-Romans. Others are killed in more merciful ways. After two or three days, the weight of the body makes breathing more difficult. Death comes, caused by suffocation and heart failure.

Quite a few spectators were at the Place of the Skull, mostly because of Jesus. Clumps of the scribes, elders, and chief priests were standing around and watching with an air of triumph. John told me that they were the ones who had been his enemies and had plotted his death.

Now they were sneering at him, shouting, "Look at him! He says he saved others. Let him save himself, if he's the Messiah! . . . Come down from the cross now—and we'll all believe! . . . He said, 'I'm God's Son.' So let God deliver him!"

People passing by added their insults: "Come down, if you're the Son of God! Save yourself!"

Even Hassen began to mock him with the same sort of taunts: "Oh, Messiah, great Messiah! Save yourself, and us too!"

Then I heard Father protest, "Hassen, don't you fear God, even now? We've been condemned and will soon die. We deserve it because of what we've done. But this man's done nothing wrong."

Then he added, "Jesus, remember me when you come into your kingdom."

I had felt ashamed to be the daughter of a thief. But now I felt proud of my father and of his courage.

Jesus struggled to turn his head to look at my father. "Yes—I will. Today you'll be with me in paradise."

I looked at Mary, who had taken in every word. "Who *is* your son?" I asked. "Is he really the Son of God, the Messiah?"

"Yes. God told me so before his birth. But I haven't yet understood what that means. I don't know how God is working now. I no longer hope for the miracle such as the scribes are mockingly calling for. He's going to die up there. But why? Why?"

It was about noon, and great black clouds began to roll in over Jerusalem from the west. The winds swept them along, then dropped them there. They blocked the sun and changed the day to night. It was scary.

I tried to listen to Mary and John and some women who had joined them. They were discussing what might happen now that their expectations of a bright future for them and for Jesus were crumbling to dust. They could see nothing good ahead.

Then Jesus called his mother and John to come closer. Soon they returned. "Just like always, he's thinking of others, even in his pain," she told us. "He's asked John to be as my son and take care of me, and me to be as his mother."

"I think you should come with me when . . . when we leave here," John invited Mary. "My brother and I have a house in Jerusalem, you know. Marcus and Joanna, you should come too, at least for now. While we were over there, your father told Jesus about you—that you'll be left alone, and I offered to take you with me."

I hardly knew what to say. We weren't used to kindness from others. Suddenly the darkness deepened and hushed our talking. An unearthly silence enveloped everything. Then we heard a shout, Jesus crying out, "It's finished! Father, I give my spirit into your hands!"

A rumble, a mighty crushing and grinding noise, rose from the earth as it shook underfoot. It heaved and trembled and split open. People were screaming with terror from the earthquake.

Then the earth slowly calmed itself and was still. The black clouds parted and began to drift away. We could see the three crosses now. The man in the middle was dead. Jesus had spoken his last words and died.

The onlookers changed their tune now. They were afraid and hurried off toward their homes, muttering, "Oh, what have we done? . . . God is showing his anger toward us."

Even the centurion, the leader of the soldiers, was affected and said to everyone who'd listen, "He must have been an innocent man—truly a Son of God!"

A strange man came up to our small group and introduced himself. "I'm Joseph from Arimathea. Some of you may know me. I'm going to go now to Pilate and ask for permission to take Jesus' body for burial. Otherwise, bodies are left there to rot and to be eaten by vultures and animals.

"I have a new tomb hewn from the rock, near here." He pointed to the next hill. "That's where we'll put the Master. I'll bring the linen cloth, too, to wrap the body."

The soldiers wouldn't let us get too near, but Marcus and I went as close as we could to Father. He was still alive but was having trouble breathing.

"Father, you're very brave and we love you," I sobbed. "We'll stay with Jesus' friend, John. I'm sure we'll . . ." I was crying too much to finish what I was saying.

Father struggled to talk. "Sorry I didn't do better for you. . . . Believe in Jesus. You'll be okay. . . . Now, please . . . go."

We backed up a little. Just then a military messenger came up to the band of soldiers on watch. We were near enough to hear his report: "The Jewish leaders don't want these men to be dying here when their holy day begins in an hour. So you're to speed things up by breaking their legs."

We watched in horror as the soldiers got up. The one who had driven the nails into the prisoners' wrists and heels took his heavy mallet and pounded Hassen's legs, cracking the bones. When his legs could no longer support his upper body, he could no longer breathe, and soon he died. They came to do the same to Father.

"It's better this way," I told Marcus. "It'll be better than for him to suffer so horribly for days, won't it?"

He nodded, but we turned away. We couldn't bear to look.

We heard the sounds of the bones breaking. We heard his loud, shuddering gasps for breath. Then, nothing. It was over.

The soldiers saw that Jesus was already dead, but one of them stuck a spear into him anyway.

Joseph from Arimathea had returned with a man named Nicodemus and a couple of servants. They were unfastening the ropes and removing the nails which held Jesus' body to the cross. Then they covered him with a white cloth.

I stood there, unable to think, unable to have the least idea of what we could do for Father. Would we have to leave him for the birds and dogs, as Joseph had said?

Then Joseph came up to us. "John has told me of your situation. My servants will carry your father's body to my tomb as well. I think Jesus would approve of them being in the same tomb—since he told your father they would soon be together in paradise."

I could tell you much more. But my aim is to report what I witnessed the day our Lord was crucified.

Let me add this yet. I did not see Jesus again after his resurrection, but I did see the tomb later that Easter Sunday morning. Some women went with me to help wrap Father's body in a linen cloth with a few spices.

We did care for my father's body as planned, but we also clearly saw the place where Jesus' body had been laid. It was empty except for the cloth he had been wrapped in. And I heard the true stories from some of the others who actually saw him.

We know Jesus lives!

14

You Can Know Jesus

by Emma of Emmaus

I've known how to spin for as long as I can remember. It's almost second nature to me.

Without thinking, while I'm sitting or walking around the house or talking, in my left hand I hold up some clean, carded wool. At the same time, my right hand twirls the spindle and stretches and spins out the wool from the pile always at hand, or from my shoulder pouch, into thread. This I wind around the spindle, then pluck up more wool from the pile always at hand, or from my shoulder pouch, to continue the process.

Our family business is spinning, dying, and weaving cloth from wool—and then selling it. My part is to help with spinning, but I can't do all of it.

For the last couple of years, since I was fourteen, I've also had the job of collecting the thread from the other women who spin for us. Then I pay them according to the amount and quality of their production.

My brother Cleopas buys the fleeces and oversees those who clean and prepare the wool for spinning. But his favorite task is to make the dyes and then to personally dye the thread. For the last two years, he's had to oversee the weavers as well and then sell our finely spun and woven wool cloth.

We've had these extra jobs to do since our brother Thomas left home to be a follower of Jesus. Here I need to go back and tell a bit about how that happened.

Our father had begun the business. My twin brothers, Thomas and Cleopas, had been working along with Father. They took it over when Father died four years ago. Mother had already been gone for six years.

Things went along well in our cloth business, and I helped more and more with the spinning as I grew older. We were fortunate to have my Aunt Dinah (Father's sister) living with us to be in charge of household affairs.

Then one day Thomas arrived back home in Emmaus (seven miles west of Jerusalem) from a selling trip to Galilee. He was all excited, a condition unusual for him.

"I think the Messiah has come at last! In Galilee everyone's talking about him. His name is Jesus—that means Savior, you know. I saw and heard him twice myself.

"As you're aware, I'm usually skeptical about such things. But his teaching and preaching are like nothing I've ever heard before. And he's been doing miraculous healing of the sick—even of leprosy and blindness! I saw it myself!"

147

"How about the cloth? Did you find time to sell any?" asked Cleopas impatiently.

I thought maybe he was a bit jealous of Thomas's enthusiasm for Jesus. They were very close as twins and up to now had shared everything.

"Yes. Nearly all our usual customers bought, and I found a few new ones. But that's not important, compared to the fact that the Messiah has come!"

"*Maybe* the Messiah has come," responded Cleopas. "Maybe some gullible people *think* he's come."

"You'll see," Thomas assured us. "He and his four friends, fishermen from Bethsaida, are going to stop here this week on their way to Jerusalem. I invited them."

Cleopas wasn't too happy about that, but what could he do? However, that short overnight visit of Jesus, Peter, Andrew, James, and John changed our lives. We (Aunt Dinah, Cleopas, and I) were so impressed by Jesus that after they left, we accused Thomas of only telling us the half!

To me, Jesus was a puzzle that I could only begin to understand. His eyes were deeply kind, yet could look piercingly into our inner thoughts and motives. Toward each person he was profoundly loving and caring, but underneath was a rocklike firmness.

His mouth curved in gentle, laughing humor, yet he was completely serious, too. He was a lovable and loving human being, but his character was like God's.

That evening Jesus asked Thomas to go with him and the others on a tour of preaching and teaching throughout Galilee, his home area. We all—including Cleopas—were thrilled and proud to have our brother chosen by Jesus, even though it meant rearranging our work responsibilities for the cloth business.

During the next three years, Cleopas and I went to Jerusalem whenever we knew Jesus and his disciples would be there on one of their visits.

Jesus had many disciples, but twelve of them were chosen as his special friends and assistants, including Thomas. These visits to Jerusalem were usually at a feast time. Often we would find Jesus in a temple portico sharing the gospel of God's kingdom with any who would listen. Thus we learned to know Jesus and his teaching better and were more and more drawn to both.

We also became aware that each time Jesus came to Jerusalem, the opposition of our religious leaders increased. Tension was mounting. This was worrisome.

Yet, as Cleopas said, "It may be necessary, probably even good. Then when the crunch comes, he'll step in to take over as Messiah-King. Jesus will reestablish our religion in its rightful place, minus all the traditions which have hindered its progress. And we are counting on him to chase the Romans from the land which, by God's promise, belongs to us."

We would be there to see it all! Perhaps our brother would have a special place in the government. I thought he'd be good at representing the interests of our area of the country. He would get a position for Cleopas, too—perhaps something concerned with small business enterprises like ours. Such were our dreams.

Then came that fateful Passover week. Others have told of the complex plots against Jesus, his betrayal by Judas (one of the twelve), the farce of a trial, the mockings and beatings Jesus underwent, and his crucifixion and death.

At each step we were hoping for the great moment when God's power would break forth through him to confound and destroy his enemies. But at each step, that hope diminished, and with his death came the death of our hope.

Cleopas and I were there at the crucifixion, with his other acquaintances, watching. Thomas, like most of the twelve, was in hiding for fear he would be crucified with his leader. Our despair matched the darkness which shrouded the sky.

Our family business donated the cloths which Joseph and Nicodemus used to wrap Jesus' body for burial.

There's the old saying "Misery loves company." At any rate, we went with Thomas plus the other disciples and acquaintances who gathered secretly at John's house, and there we passed a dreary and nearly silent Sabbath together.

After the Sabbath some of the women from the group went early Sunday morning to the tomb to provide some more embalming spices for Jesus' body. Soon they were back, breathless and trembling.

One woman managed to gasp out, "There's no body in the tomb! We saw an angel who said, 'He's risen!' "

"That's right!" exclaimed another. "There were two angels! And they said, 'He did as he told you he'd do—on the third day he rose from the dead!' "

"That's a likely story!" snorted Thomas.

"You women and your imaginations!" groaned another.

Peter and John, however, looked at each other, got up, and ran out the door.

When they returned, John had a curious expression on his face, almost a smile.

Peter spoke. "It's true—there's no body. The cloths he was wrapped in were lying there, empty. And the cloth that had been tied around his head—it was lying by itself, all rolled up!"

Some said one thing, and some another: "What does it mean? . . . Well then, where's the body? . . . The women told us the stone was rolled back. How did that happen? . . . Peter and John didn't see any angels. The women must have dreamed about them. . . . Alive? Don't you believe it! He'd be here with his friends if that were true."

No one suspected or thought or believed the real truth.

About mid-afternoon that Sunday, Cleopas and I set out for Emmaus. There was work waiting to be done, and we didn't know of anything further we could do in Jerusalem. We walked and talked, once more hashing over the events, but coming to no conclusion.

A man walking alone fell into step alongside us. "You seemed to be having quite a discussion," he commented. "What were you talking about?"

Cleopas replied, "You must be the only one within miles who doesn't know about the things that have happened!"

"What things?"

So Cleopas explained everything, what had been our hopes, Jesus' trial and death, the women's report, and the empty tomb.

The man shook his head as if amazed. "Oh, how

foolish you are! How reluctant and slow to believe the prophets! Don't you realize that the Messiah had to go through all this suffering to bring peace between God and humans?"

Then he explained from Moses and the prophets all the passages about the Messiah. We had our ideas, scriptural we thought, about what the Messiah should do, how he should act. How could we have forgotten or ignored words like these from Isaiah?

> He was wounded for transgressions,
>   crushed for our iniquities;
> upon him was the punishment that made us whole,
>   and by his bruises we are healed.
> All we like sheep have gone astray;
>   we have all turned to our own way,
> and the Lord has laid on him
>   the iniquity of us all. . . .
> They made his grave with the wicked
>   and his tomb with the rich,
> although he had done no violence,
>   and there was no deceit in his mouth. . . .
> He . . . was numbered with the transgressors;
>   yet he bore the sin of many,
> and made intercession for the transgressors.

The Messiah was God's servant, sent to suffer and die for our sins! If this was God's plan, Jesus could be the Messiah after all!

We were so engrossed that we didn't realize we'd arrived at Emmaus.

"Please stay with us," Cleopas invited him. "It's nearly evening. Eat with us and spend the night. We have little enough to offer you for what you showed us about the teachings of the prophets."

The stranger accepted, and we soon sat down to our simple evening meal of bread, goat cheese, fruit, and wine, served by Aunt Dinah.

We were surprised when our visitor acted like the host. He took the bread, prayed, broke it, and served it. At that moment, we recognized our visitor. He was the Lord!

"Jesus, it's you!" Cleopas shouted with joy. "We should have known!"

But he was no longer there. Where he'd been sitting, there was only the broken bread and the empty chair.

"Oh, why didn't we realize sooner that it was the Lord?" moaned Cleopas.

"Perhaps because his cloak partly hid his face as we were walking," I guessed.

"Then too, we were walking westward and the evening sun was glaring in our eyes," added Cleopas.

"But we should have recognized his voice!" I insisted. "We should have recognized his way of explaining the Scriptures."

"We should have believed the women! We should have remembered what he told us about rising from the dead!" Cleopas exclaimed.

"Did you see the scars from the nails on his hands when he broke the bread?" I asked. "I think that's what made me realize . . ."

"Well, all this discussion isn't important! What counts is that we've seen and talked to the Lord. He's alive! I think we should go back to Jerusalem yet tonight and let the others know what's happened!"

So we quickly finished our meal and set out to retrace our route in the dusk of the evening. We found a great change in the sad and skeptical people we'd left only hours earlier.

They greeted us: "The Lord really *is* alive! Peter's seen him!"

When we told our story, they became even more excited. What would happen next? Some were wildly expecting the same sort of scene to develop for which we had been hoping—Jesus as king and the Romans routed.

Cleopas was trying to explain the different Messiah which Jesus had shown us from the Scriptures, one who accepts suffering for the sake of God's glorious kingdom.

Just then he was interrupted by a voice: "Peace be with you."

The Lord was *there,* right there among us—and his word was "peace," not armed revolution.

Even though everyone had heard that he was alive, their first reactions were terror and doubt. Jesus calmed them with his words, assuring them it was really he and not a ghost.

Then he calmed them with his actions, showing his scarred hands. He asked for some food and ate it. After that he began to explain some of the same Scriptures he had already discussed with Cleopas and me.

"Where's Thomas?" I whispered to my brother.

"Philip told me he was so depressed and downhearted he only wanted to be alone," Cleopas replied. "I don't know where he's gone, Emma, but you know him. Now that he's missed seeing Jesus, he'll have a hard time believing what any of us tell him. He'll want to see Jesus himself."

Thomas did see him later, but that's another story.

That night, the Lord also told us that his Spirit would give us power so we could tell others about him. At the time, we still didn't realize what he meant. We wrongly assumed that now that he'd returned to life, he would be with us as before.

For a few weeks, he did appear to us now and then, but too soon that was over. He, the Son of God, returned to heaven to his Father. Yet he remained with us and in us through the Spirit.

Many of you haven't seen Jesus, but we have, and as we report, you can see with us. We who believe in Jesus the Messiah-King are now his body, the church, continuing his work on earth.

Bible Texts Behind These Stories

Chapter 1. Psalm 19:1-2; 23:1-6; Micah 5:2; Matthew 1:18—2:18; Luke 1:26-38; 2:1-20.

Chapter 2. Exodus 30:11-16; Psalm 40:6-8; Jeremiah 7:11; Micah 6:6-8; Matthew 21:12-17; Mark 11:15-19; Luke 2:39-52; John 2:13-22; 9:1-3.

Chapter 3. Isaiah 61:1-2; Matthew 12:43-50; 13:53-58; 21:28-32; 23:2; Mark 2:1-2, 15 (perhaps Jesus even had a house at Capernaum; see *NRSV* note, "his house"); 3:31-35; 6:1-6; Luke 4:14-30; 8:19-21; 11:24-25; 15:8-10; John 2:1-11.

Chapter 4. Matthew 6:25-33; 8:14-17; 13:1-3, 45-50; Mark 1:16-34; 4:1-2; Luke 4:31—5:11; 12:22-28.

Chapter 5. Matthew 8:23-34; Mark 4:35—5:20; Luke 8:22-39.

Chapter 6. Leviticus 15:19-30; Matthew 9:18-26; Mark 5:21-45; Luke 8:40-56.

Chapter 7. Matthew 5:43-48; 6:2-4; 7:3-5, 21-27; 14:13-

21; Mark 6:30-44; Luke 6:37-49; 9:10-17; John 6:1-35.

Chapter 8. Matthew 17:14-21; Mark 9:14-29; Luke 9:37-43; John 12:6.

Chapter 9. Matthew 23:1-36; Mark 7:1-23; Luke 11:9-54.

Chapter 10. Matthew 9:9-13; 18:12-14; Mark 2:13-17; 10:46-52; Luke 5:27-32; 15:1-7; 18:35-43; 19:1-10.

Chapter 11. Psalm 8:2; Isaiah 56:7; Zechariah 9:9; Matthew 21:1-17; Mark 11:1-11, 15-19; Luke 19:29-45; John 12:9-19.

Chapter 12. Matthew 21:23-27; 26:3-5, 14-16, 36-75; 27:1-10; Mark 11:27-33; 14:1-2, 10-11, 26-72; Luke 20:1-8; 22:1-6, 39-42; John 13:21-30; 18:1-28; Acts 1:15-20; 3:1-22.

Chapter 13. Matthew 27:24-61; Mark 15:16-47; Luke 10:29-37; 23:13—24:12; John 19:27—20:10.

Chapter 14. Isaiah 53:1-12; Luke 23:49—24:49; John 11:16; 20:1-29; 21:2.

The Author

Marian Hostetler returned to the USA the summer of 1993 from a five-year stint of teaching English as a foreign language for Eastern Mennonite Missions in a secondary school in Djibouti, a small African country bordered by Ethiopia, Somalia, and the Red Sea.

This Orrville, Ohio, native also taught in Somalia for a year, in Algeria with Mennonite Board of Missions (1961-70), and served for short terms in France, Ivory Coast, Benin, and Nepal. She has traveled in the Middle East and worked as a volunteer on archaeological digs in Cyprus and Carthage.

Hostetler is now living in Elkhart, Indiana, where she is a member of the Belmont Mennonite Church, and where she taught at Concord Schools from 1970-88. Beside teaching and writing, she enjoys reading, painting, sewing, and music.

In total, Marian Hostetler served overseas as a teacher for sixteen years, mainly in Africa. She enjoys putting this experience into fiction for junior age children, as she did in *African Adventure, Journey to Jerusalem,* and *Fear in Algeria.* Yet two of her mystery stories take place in the United States: *Secret in the City* and *Mystery at the Mall.*

Several of her books have been translated into other languages: Finnish, French, German, Portuguese, and Spanish. One of these books, *They Loved Their Enemies,* is a collection of true stories from Africa.

Hostetler enjoyed the Bible study and imagination it took to produce the stories in *We Knew Paul.* Hence, she decided to use a similar format for the stories in *We Knew Jesus.*

She says, "Although some of the people in these stories are the writer's creation, yet they fit their place in the Gospel accounts of Jesus. There must have been young people like them, and they became real to me as I was telling their stories."

These two books reflect Hostetler's interest in the Bible and in bringing it to life in stories that can excite not only young people but older ones as well.